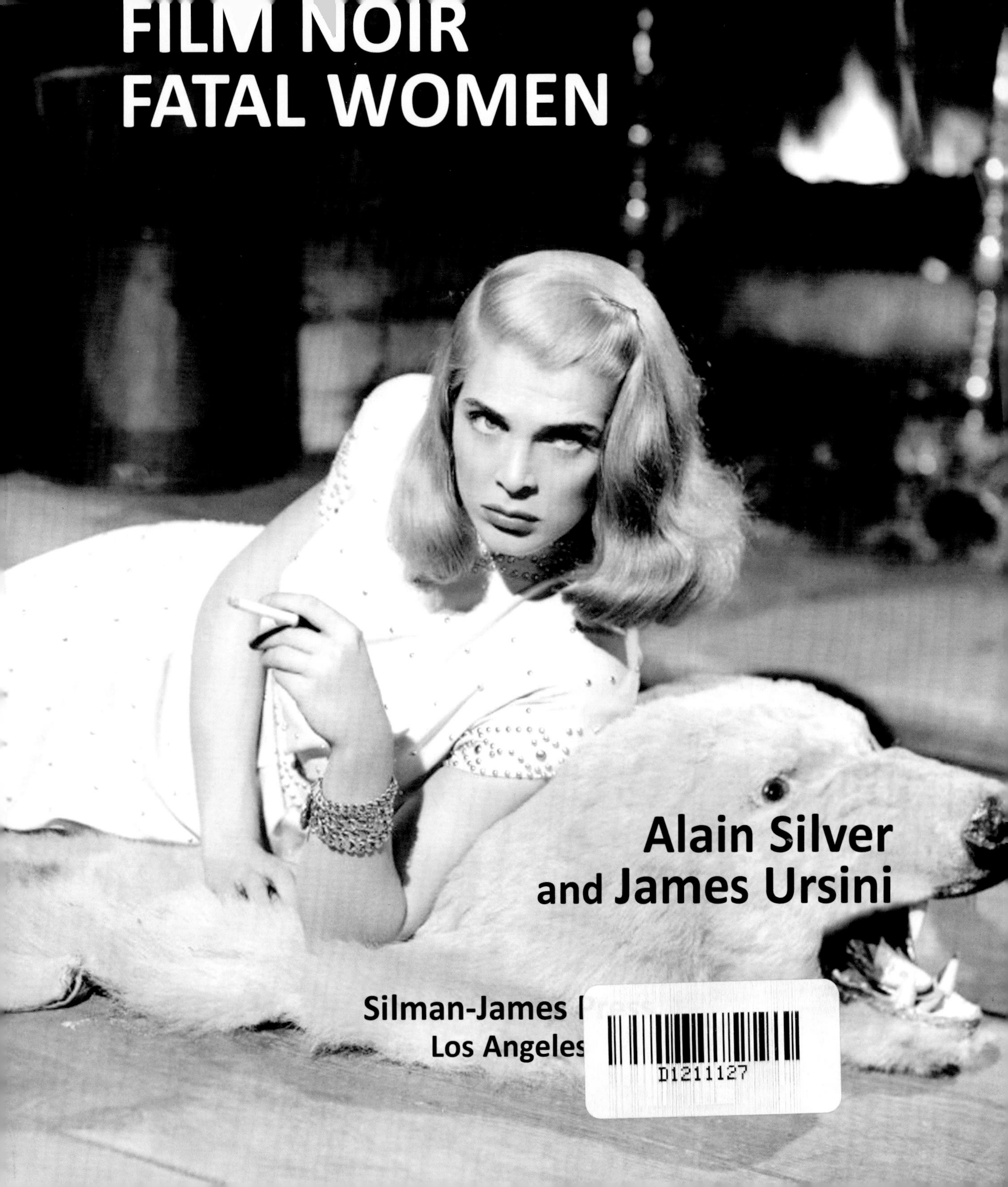
FILM NOIR
FATAL WOMEN
Alain Silver
and James Ursini
Silman-James
Los Angeles

Acknowledgments

Stills and graphics, most of which are from the personal collections of the authors, are reproduced courtesy of Allied Artists, Columbia, Lippert, MGM, Paramount, PRC, RKO, Selznick, 20th Century Fox, United Artists, Universal, Warner Bros. and others.

Special thanks must go to our frequent collaborators Linda Brookover, Dominique Mainon, Robert Porfirio, and Elizabeth Ward for a large part of the work underlying this volume. We are also grateful to Richard Deming and Walter Hill for their generous comments and to our editors Jim Fox and Gwen Feldman.

Published by
Silman-James Press
Los Angeles

ISBN: 978-1-935247-25-8

Library of Congress Cataloging-in-Publication Data

Names: Silver, Alain, 1947- author. | Ursini, James, author.

Title: Film noir fatal women / Alain Silver and James Ursini.

Description: Los Angeles : Silman-James Press, 2021. | Includes index. |

Identifiers: LCCN 2021030222 | ISBN 9781935247258 (paperback)

Subjects: LCSH: Femmes fatales in motion pictures. | Film noir--History and criticism.

Classification: LCC PN1995.9.F44 S555 2021 | DDC 791.43/6522--dc23

LC record available at https://lccn.loc.gov/2021030222

Book and cover design by Alain Silver.

Front cover: Faith Domergue.

Back cover: Gloria Grahame.

Frontispiece: Lizabeth Scott smokes on a bearskin in *Desert Fury* (1947).

FILM NOIR
FATAL WOMEN

By the same Authors

David Lean and His Films (1974)
More Things Than Are Dreamt Of (1994)
What Ever Happened to Robert Aldrich? (1995)
Film Noir Reader (1996)
The Noir Style (1999)
Film Noir Reader 2 (1999)
Horror Film Reader (2000)
Film Noir Reader 3 (with Robert Porfirio, 2002)
Film Noir Reader 4 (2004)
Film Noir (Taschen, 2004)
L.A. Noir The City as Character (2005)
Roger Corman: Metaphysics on a Shoestring (2006)
Gangster Film Reader (2007)
Film Noir The Encyclopedia (4th Edition, 2010)
The Vampire Film from Nosferatu *to* True Blood (2011)
Film Noir The Directors (2012)
Film Noir Graphics: Where Danger Lives (2012)
The Zombie Film (2014)
American Neo-Noir (2015)
Film Noir Compendium (2016)
The Film Noir Jigsaw: Critical Perspectives on the Classic Period (2016)
Film Noir Light and Shadow (2017)
Film Noir Prototypes (2018)

Also by Alain Silver

Robert Aldrich (with Elizabeth Ward, 1979)
The Film Director's Team (with Elizabeth Ward, 1983)
Raymond Chandler's Los Angeles (with Elizabeth Ward, 1987)
The Samurai Film (3rd Edition, 2005)
James Wong Howe The Camera Eye (2010)
Movies Without Baggage (2022)

Also by James Ursini

The Fabulous Life and Times of Preston Sturges An American Dreamer (1976)
The Modern Amazons: Warrior Women on Screen (with Dominique Mainon, 2006)
Cinema of Obsession (with Dominique Mainon, 2007)
Femme Fatale (with Dominique Mainon, 2009)
Directors on the Edge (2011)

Contents

Ava Gardner in *The Killers* (1946)

Preface

As many of our readers already know, our work on film noir goes back quite a few years. Collectively, we have written or edited more than a few books about the classic period, its Neo-noir aftermath, and specific topics from *The Noir Style* to the city as character in *L.A. Noir*. This volume is, in fact, our sixteenth focused on some aspect of film noir.

While we hope that our critical approach has been consistent and mostly focused on the style that we believe defines film noir, in the beginning that often meant settling for less than optimal illustrations. Often we would have to be satisfied with acquiring any publicity still for a given title, whether or not it replicated a moment that was under discussion anywhere in the text. The other significant constraint in earlier days was the dependence on others, on design professionals who would take our text—which in the first edition of *Film Noir The Encyclopedia* started out hand-written on legal pads and index cards—and as many images as we could cobble together to create the finished book. Back then, capturing a shot from a movie required a special apparatus: a quasi-camera with a metal front plate that held frames of 16mm prints in front of a photoflood for timed exposure on a roll of fine grain negative. The process time consuming—capturing, developing, and printing frames from *Kiss Me Deadly* for a 1975 *Film Comment* article took many hours—and typical results were low-contrast, low-resolution prints.

Thankfully times have changed. The first *Film Noir Reader* in 1996 reprinted the *Kiss Me Deadly* piece and also included an excerpt from Robert Porfirio's ground-breaking dissertation, a visual analysis of the long-take, hat-factory robbery in *The Killers*. Higher resolution scans of the same vintage frame enlargements (Bob had made his in the 1970s also), enhanced both the sharpness and contrast. It would take another two decades of technological development to permit us quickly to swap out those vintage frame enlargements with image captures from high-quality DVD releases from Criterion when we reprinted those essays in 2016's *Film Noir Compendium*. Now with Blu-ray releases a selected frame can sharply fill the width of an 8x10 page.

For over twenty years, desktop publishing systems have allowed us to design our books. Initially that still meant printing out pages and sending images out for third-party compositing. Now we can lay out every page (and the covers as well) and deliver finished PDF files to a publisher via email. For *The Noir Style*, with its visual analysis masquerading as a coffee-table book, method defined the design. Groups of related images defined themes and sidebar sections discussed precursors and motifs. But we were restricted: if we could not find a quality still for a given title, we could not include it.

Most recently and whenever possible we have favored images over text to analyze the noir style. For the first time in this newest volume, the majority of its pages use that approach, incorporating sidebars and motifs and sometimes combining scene stills and frames as in the "faces of Lizabeth Scott" on pages 124-125.

As always we hope that the quality of the images within leads you back to the movie fatal women and their films.

Alla Nazimova in *Salome* (1923).

Deadly Precursors

The fatal woman is an ancient part of the collective unconscious in art and literature with some of her earliest appearances being found in the Bible. Its first woman, Eve, becomes a fatal one as she entices Adam to sin. In Talmudic lore the rebellious figure of Lilith is even older, the original woman who rejected both the dominance of Adam and God and was vilified as a demon who steals newborns. However in a post-feminist world she has been adopted as an empowering icon.

The French epithet "femme fatale" literally means "deadly woman," which understates the human embodiment of lust and peril, the allure of sex and death that makes these creatures fascinating both literally and metaphorically. The fatal woman is typically a sleek and sensuous creature, who can pose both physical and emotional danger to her victims. Unlike the more aggressive archetype of a female fighter or warrior, the fatal woman's weapons are more subtle and elusive. She would use poison rather than a gun, employ guile and seduction rather than physical power to achieve her aims.

While fatal women may not be as overtly violent, like their warrior counterparts they undermine patriarchal structures. Their motives are more likely personal than patriotic, working from behind the scenes and more to fulfill their own needs or transgressive desires rather than any ideals. They are spies such as the alluring Mata Hari, as opposed to warrior women like the Valkyrie Brunhild. Such a woman slowly strips her victims of their moral values, their friends and often their wealth. She is sexually insatiable and may even love her victims in her own way, but that doesn't stop her from exploiting their obsession. The male's resulting exhaustion leads to confusion and inability to make sensible or rational decisions. Men who associate with a fatal woman risk being humiliated, driven to despair, or even killed.

The fatal woman has had many forms. She may be the Egyptian Sphinx, half-human, half-animal, or the Bible's teenage seductress Salome or World War I spy Mata Hari or the evil Queen in *Snow White*. As rulers fatal women range from Cleopatra, the Roman empress Messalina, or the Byzantine queen Theodora to the much maligned Renaissance princess Lucrezia Borgia and the misunderstood second wife of Henry VIII, Anne Boleyn. Many of these women have been transformed into femme fatales by male historians, simply for exercising power much like their male contemporaries did.

The archetype In fin-de-siècle work of Decadent writers and artists such as Baudelaire, Gustave Moreau, Théophile Gautier, Oscar Wilde, Pierre Louÿs, or Octave Mirbeau evolved into the proto-typical "Fatal Woman" of the American cinema in the silent and pre-Code eras, where American audiences hungry for glamour lived vicariously through these radiant and dangerous characters. European filmmakers opted for more nuanced characterizations.

All of these sources ultimately distilled and blended into the "Fatal Woman" of classic period film noir.

Above, Theda Bara in *The Soul of Buddha* (1918). Opposite, Alla Nazimova in *Camille* (1921).

The early days of the cinema—the days before 1934, when the office that administered the Motion Picture Production Code decided to enforce the puritanical rules that had been in place for almost a decade—were among the most fertile for the fatal woman. Her image was formed then and her influence established.

Theda Bara

Theda Bara (born Theodosia Goodman) epitomizes the exoticism inextricably linked to the image of the fatal woman. Her dark Sephardic appearance radiated the same combination of menace and allure which characterized the fatal women of history and fin-de-siecle literature. In addition, the publicity agents at Fox, drawing on their own knowledge of Decadent literature, created a tantalizing biography for their first real star. According to the studio Theda Bara (an anagram of the words "arab death") was the daughter of a French artist and an Egyptian concubine. She was born in the Sahara desert and possessed supernatural powers. They posed her in scanty costumes, often next to or on top of the bones of her latest "victim." They even coined the term "vamp" to describe her (drawn from the famous Rudyard Kipling poem "The Vampire"), a term that would become part of the language within a decade. Bara's character possesses no supernatural power, but her ability to lure men into cooperating with their own course of destruction was equally lethal.

Theda Bara was one of the first film actresses to take on the roles of such formidable literary and historical fatal women as Carmen, Camille, Salome, Madame Du Barry, and Cleopatra, although, sadly, copies of those films to date have been lost. We do, however, still have her debut film as a star, *A Fool There Was* (1915), which she described in her own words (using a false, thick foreign accent in keeping with her studio-created persona) to aspiring journalist Louella Parsons as "a charnel house of men's dead hopes and withered ambitions...this vampire of mine possesses only one good or decent quality, her courage."

Nazimova

Russian theatrical star Alla Nazimova was among the first actresses who benefited from Hollywood's interest in importing its fatal women rather than home-growing them as they had done with Bara. To Americans at the turn of the twentieth century Europe represented the decadent old world filled with debauchery and corruption. One can see this reflected clearly in the novels of American writers like Henry James. It was in addition the birthplace of the fatal woman in literature. So why not take advantage of this perceived ethos as well as Europe's own highly developed and artistic worlds of cinema and theater?

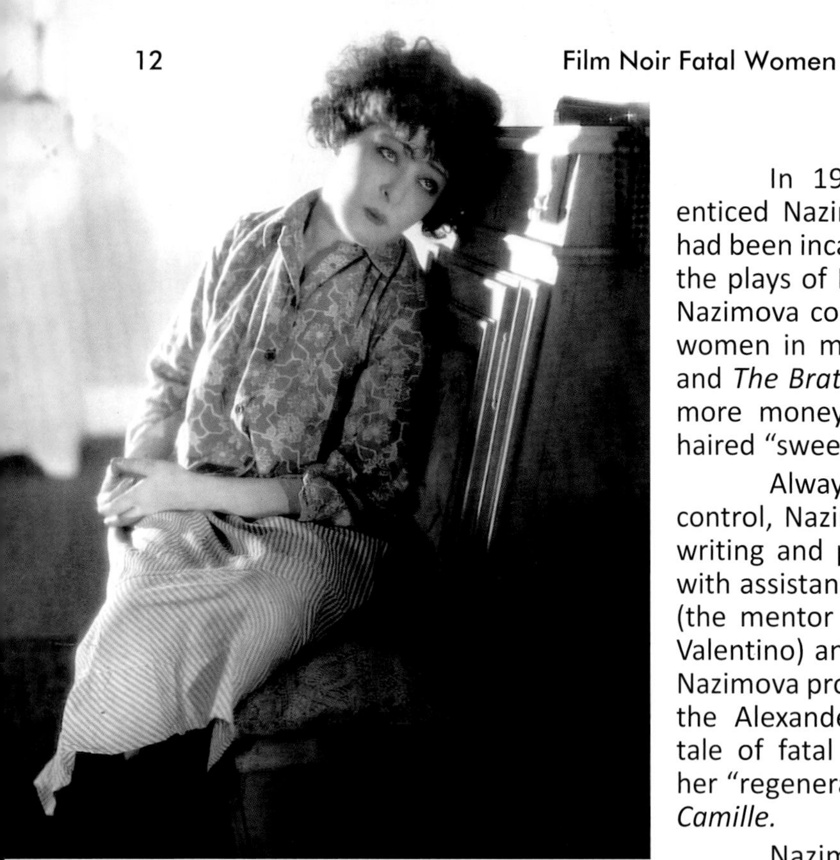

In 1915 Producer Lewis J. Selznick enticed Nazimova from the stage where she had been incarnating strong modern women in the plays of Ibsen and Chekhov. In Hollywood Nazimova continued her portrayal of complex women in movies like *Revelation* (1918, left) and *The Brat* (1919). By 1919 she was making more money per film than America's curly-haired "sweetheart" Mary Pickford.

Always seeking to expand her creative control, Nazimova began to participate in the writing and production of her films. In 1921, with assistance from noted writer June Mathis (the mentor of the film's male star, Rudolph Valentino) and art director Natacha Rambova, Nazimova produced her own stylized version of the Alexander Dumas (fils) world-renowned tale of fatal woman Marguerite/Camille and her "regeneration" through the power of love, *Camille.*

Nazimova's cinematic Waterloo was her 1923 adaptation of Oscar Wilde's decadent play *Salome.* Based on the Biblical story of the teenage vixen, her seduction of her uncle Herod, and her obsession with the beautiful but pure John the Baptist, Wilde's play had been met only with derision and legal action during its early performances. Nazimova adapted the play with Natacha Rambova (who also designed the costumes and sets), remaining faithful to the spirit of the piece. The designs were largely inspired by art nouveau artist Aubrey Beardsley's drawings for the publication of the play and were dazzling but possibly too bizarre for American audiences.

In addition Nazimova was moving into middle age and probably not the best choice for the role of the petulant and lustful teenager Salome. The film was a financial and critical failure. This fact combined with the changing tastes of modern Jazz Age audiences gently pushed Nazimova into retirement from the screen.

Clara Bow

Clara Bow (opposite) was "the It girl" of the 1920s, the name given to her by writer Elinor Glyn, who picked her for the film adaptation of her book *It* in 1927. Years before through her own efforts and personality, Bow had already become the apotheosis of the jazz-age flapper. When Glyn had placed her seal of approval on Bow, she already combined a naughty-girl quality with an overpowering drive to achieve her goals. She was the fatal child-woman of the 1920s, sure of her sexuality and the power it gave her. She had herself grown up a victim of poverty and abuse and became a working class archetype, a woman who knew how to exploit the patriarchy to carve out her own place in society.

Bow really began formulating her screen persona when she joined forces with producer B. P. Schulberg in 1923. Although Schulberg overworked and underpaid Bow (she made over forty films within four years), he gave her the freedom to develop her natural exuberance and playful sexuality, which led to her stardom and Paramount's decision to buy Schulberg's company simply to add Bow to their roster of stars.

Bow's first huge hit was in 1926, *Mantrap*, directed by her newest mentor and lover Victor Fleming (he would direct her again the next year in the provocative *Hula*). Fleming was devoted to Bow and spoke with adulation of her natural qualities before the camera.

Call Her Savage (1932, above) is in many ways Bow's best film and unfortunately her second to last effort. It has only recently been rediscovered and restored and so has not received the attention that many other pre-Code films have. For it is among the most daring of that string of liberated films which directly preceded the crackdown by the Production Code Office in 1934.

Bow's salary was unsurpassed by any star of the period. Bow, however, became disillusioned with the Hollywood factory and retired in 1933. Mental illness haunted Bow the rest of her life, much as it had her mother. She died in 1965 with little fanfare from a movie business which had largely forgotten her.

Brigitte Helm

Although Europe, as noted, supplied the archetype of the fatal woman through the literature and art of the Decadent movement, the cinema itself produced far fewer examples of lethal ladies. European cinema has always had a predilection for more dimensional characters and therefore has often opted for a more naturalistic approach to characterization and story while the American cinema has excelled in the molding of genres like the Western or the gangster film along with their attendant archetypes and icons.

Although mostly forgotten today except for her searing performance as the two Marias in Fritz Lang's *Metropolis,* Helm might have been an international movie goddess at the level of Dietrich or Garbo; but she showed insufficient interest in obtaining the role of Lola Lola in *The Blue Angel*, which went, of course, to Dietrich and made her a star. Again when offered the part of the bride in James Whale's *Bride of Frankenstein*, she refused. After these two career errors she stayed in Germany until her disgust with the Nazis and their control of the film industry, prompted early retirement from movies and self-exile to Switzerland.

Nevertheless, Brigitte Helm's mastery of the fatal woman is unrivaled in several of the films which have survived from the silent and early sound German cinema. Her tall sinuous dancer's body, blond hair, aquiline nose, piercing eyes, and full arrogant lips inspired critics to dub her "the Teutonic Goddess." And in many ways Helm paved the way for actresses like Dietrich and Garbo in their transformation of a deadly female from vamp to goddess.

In 1932 distinguished director G.W. Pabst (*Pandora's Box*) cast Helm in his adaptation of the story of the lost city of Atlantis and its goddess Antinea (below) in *L'Atlantide (Queen of Atlantis*, English title). In the North African desert Officer Saint-Avit of the Foreign Legion stumbles with his troop on the lost city of Atlantis, ruled by the narcissistic Antinea. The scenes in the city itself are staged as if the product of a hashish dream.

Antinea herself is presented like an icon, gazing longingly at herself in a mirror, hissing at an errant leopard, walking sinuously through her boudoir dressed in jewels and silk. The film is a remarkable example of the fatal woman icon to this day.

Motif - Exotic Costuming

The pose of Margaretha Geertruida "Margreet" MacLeod aka Mata Hari, in 1905 inspired the look of many fictional fatal women such as Brigitte Helm as Antinea. Among the earliest, opposite top left, was Theda Bara in *Cleopatra*.

Above, Clara Bow in *Hoopla*.

Below, Brigitte Helm in *Metropolis*.

More exotic costuming: Greta Garbo as the legendary Mata Hari, opposite and following page.

At right, in *Flesh and the Devil.*

Greta Garbo

Greta Garbo was imported from Europe to play the vamp who was redolent of the old decadent world. However, what Garbo was able to accomplish was to raise the vamp to the level of a goddess. Along with fellow émigré Marlene Dietrich she changed the image of the fatal woman as much as Clara Bow had done in the 1920s but in a completely different direction.

Garbo was the priestess of love in her films. What MGM exec Louis B. Mayer saw in her eyes when he viewed her films in Europe was not "gentleness," as he claimed, but a sensuality verging on ecstasy. Once she was imported to Hollywood from her native Sweden in 1925, the dream factory capitalized on that sensuality and produced yet another archetype of the American movies, the fatal woman as goddess, a superior being who men cannot resist worshipping in classics like *Flesh and the Devil* (1927), *Mata Hari* (1931), and *Camille* (1936).

Marlene Dietrich

Garbo's rival in the 1930s for the role of fatal woman supreme was Marlene Dietrich. The seven films Marlene Dietrich and her director Josef von Sternberg made from 1930 to 1935 (beginning with *The Blue Angel* and ending with *The Devil Is a Woman*) not only solidified the iconic status of Dietrich but also reflected the couple's own complex relationship.

The Devil Is a Woman (1935) is the last film in the Dietrich-von Sternberg oeuvre and arguably the best. The story is largely a reworking of *The Blue Angel*, even though it is based on the infamous decadent novel *The Woman and the Puppet* by Pierre Louÿs. During a festival in Spain, an aging roué and military hero, Don Pasqual (Lionel Atwill), tells of his relationship with the tempestuous and whimsical Concha (Dietrich), "the toast of Spain." Like Professor Rath in *The Blue Angel* (a young Dietrich in a classic pose, below), Don Pasqual pursues and attempts to control the free-spirited cigarette girl/performer (the allusion to *Carmen* is significant here) but predictably with little success.

Still more exotic costuming: Marlene Dietrich in *The Devil is a Woman* and a variant on the earlier von Sternberg in *Morocco* on the following page.

Anna May Wong

Women of color, it is no surprise to say, did not fare well in early Hollywood. They were usually relegated to minor stereotyped roles: servants, menial workers, or extras to give a setting authenticity. In fact when the studios took on a project which centered around characters of color, they most often cast a White actor. The most relevant example of this relates directly to Anna May Wong, the first Asian vamp of the American cinema. In 1936 when MGM was casting their adaptation of Pearl Buck's tale of Chinese peasants and their struggles, *The Good Earth*, they initially considered Wong, who was by then an international star. But they rejected her for a White actress who then went on to win the Academy Award for her performance.

Below, *Shanghai Express*: Anna May Wong as Hui-Fei in a supporting role to Dietrich's Lily in another von Sternberg collaboration. The very framing of most shots with the actresses underscores the marginalization of the Asian character.

A full-on display of Hollywood exoticism from costuming to scenic design in the posed still for *Daughter of the Dragon*.

Wong, born in 1905, grew up in the heart of the movie industry, Los Angeles, where her father ran a laundry. At an early age she became fascinated by the movies and convinced her disapproving father to allow her to audition for parts. In most of her early roles Wong incarnated the Western stereotype of what Sheridan Prasso in her book *The Asian Mystique* calls the "China Doll," the submissive, Madame Butterfly beauty. In fact at the age of seventeen Wong was cast in a rough adaptation of the Madame Butterfly story itself, *The Toll of the Sea* (1922). Her character name was appropriately Lotus Flower.

Wong was only able to break out of those roles by adapting to yet another Western stereotype—what Prasso refers to as the "Dragon Lady" image—the exotic, devious, and lethal Asian fatal woman. Although Wong naturally chafed at being typed into playing these parts over and over, they at least allowed her to express a range of emotions as well as present Asian women as possessing true independence. Douglas Fairbanks recognized this inherent strength and deep sensuality in Wong when he cast her as the rebellious and manipulative Mongol Slave in his Arabian Nights fantasy *The Thief of Bagdad* (1924). As slave to the Princess she harbors thoughts of revenge on her captors and so plots with the Mongol invaders to overthrow the kingdom of Bagdad.

In 1928 Wong decided to expand her horizons and move to Europe, where she worked on stage and in the movies. Her experience there turned her into an international star as the Europeans received her warmly. In 1929 German director E.A. Dupont (*Variety)* collaborated with Wong on a film which would secure her reputation in Europe as well as in the United States: *Piccadilly.* Wong worked extensively with Dupont on her costumes and dance routines, as she did in many of her films, and the result is a luminously erotic performance which showcases the many talents Wong possessed. In the film she plays a scullery maid, Shosho, who moves from kitchen to center stage by means of her talent as

Left, before she became a "dragon lady" Anna May Wong's first starring role in *Toll of the Sea* was as the stereotypical Asian "maiden" Lotus Flower, costumed and made-up to underscore the innocence suggested by her character name. Below, the considerably more menacing, knife-wielding Hui-Fei, restrained by Dietrich's Shanghai Lily.

Piccadilly: costume and make-up design from Anna May Wong and E.A. Dupont.

well as her ability to manipulate powerful men. She is discovered by the club owner, Wilmot (Jameson Thomas), dancing sumptuously to the delight of his employees.

Intrigued by her beauty and allure, Wilmot invites her to his office late one night to "dance" for him. We never see what occurs between them but we can guess by how she treats him throughout the rest of the film. Shosho understands the ways of the patriarchy and so plays a coy game of tease and denial like any true fatal woman, not allowing him to get too close to her until he has delivered on his promises. She dresses her surly servant/lover Jim (King Hou Chang) in her costumes, denying Wilmot the pleasure of seeing her in them until he has agreed to let her use wardrobe of her own design. She teases him by going out to pubs with him dressed in sensual furs and satins, but refuses him entry into her new apartments. She touches his mouth with her slender fingers and sharpened nails and then presses them to her own full lips, denying once again his attempt to kiss her. Only when he has featured her at his club and signed her to a long-term contract, to the chagrin of his former lover and star Mabel (Gilda Gray), does she allow him beyond the shimmering veil she places over her face to incite his lust.

In 1931 Paramount offered Wong a lucrative contract, so she returned to the U.S. and starred in an adaptation of the novel *Daughter of the Dragon* in the Sax Rohmer series centering on the incarnation of evil "yellow peril" Fu Manchu (played by the very non-Asian Warner Oland). Paramount spent thousands of dollars on Wong's costumes and allowed her input in their design.

Jean Harlow

Jean Harlow was a perfect fatal woman for the 1930s Great Depression. Even when she played middle or upper class characters, she exuded the street. Her heavy drinking and chain-smoking, her lack of underwear, her working class argot, her witty repartee, and her sometimes bawdy humor—all made her a favorite of the first half of a decade tired of the rarefied, European-influenced atmosphere of the 1920s cinema and yearning for a realism which reflected the realities, with a touch of escapism, of their own hard lives.

Harlow burst on the scene with her "boiling" performance as the sexually liberated Helen in Howard Hughes' flying epic *Hell's Angels* (1930). In the film Harlow is a very modern young Englishwoman who is the female version of the film's male roué Monte (Ben Lyon). Although she is dating his morally rigid and somewhat naïve brother Roy (James Hall), she tells the baffled Monte that this should not stand in the way of their affair. After all it is her business: "I want to be free. I want to be gay and have fun." We first see Helen in action when she rushes into the room to meet the overwhelmed Roy. She tells him that she is "boiling" and he runs his hand tentatively over her skin, his hand trembling from the heat she emits.

Hell's Angels: Jean Harlow as Helen displays considerable décolletage in a scene with Monte (Ben Lyon).

In the year after *Hell's Angels*, Harlow made a brief but memorable appearance for Warner Bros. in the watershed crime film *The Public Enemy*. Harlow's real life associations with gangsters gave an authenticity to her performance as Gwen, a "lady of leisure," whom the protagonist, gangster Tom Powers (James Cagney), spies on the street and then offers a ride to, thinking he has made another easy score. However, Gwen turns the tables on this criminal player by withholding her favors until she has established her dominance over him and driven him a little "screwy," as he tells her. When she is sure that he does not consider her just another easy woman, she mounts his lap and toys with his hair, pressing his head to her breast and calling him her "bashful boy."

Red-Headed Woman (also 1932, below) was written by Anita Loos, one of a squadron of female writers who helped develop the American cinema in its first four decades. This film is among the most sexually direct of the pre-Code films of the early 1930s. The film opens with a montage which pays homage to Loos' phenomenally successful book and screenplay, *Gentlemen Prefer Blondes,* while capitalizing on Harlow's now finely formed iconic image as she changes her hair from its famous platinum color to red, asks advice about whether her dress is transparent enough (reinforcing her reputed real-life dislike of undergarments, a trend among pre-Code screen sirens), and then reveals fishnets and a garter (which features a photo of her boss) as she discusses with her gal pal Sally (Una Merkel) how she is going to "upgrade" her life from shop girl to society dame.

Unfortunately, Harlow died in 1937 of uremic poisoning. However, by then, the Code Office had done its work on Harlow's post-1934 films and stripped them of any overt sexuality and daring content in the script stage. So like so many Pre-Code fatal woman films they became pale shadows of their pre-Code forerunners.

The Public Enemy: Jean Harlow as Helen with a long cigarette holder and seemingly unaware of the rod in the hand of Tom Powers (James Cagney).

Part One: Themes and Styles

Sirens - Dressed to Kill

Of guileful Circe too he spake, deep-skilled
In various artifice, and how he reached
With sails and oars the squalid realms of death...
Whose dreadful fate he yet, himself, escaped.

Odyssey, Book 12

As guileful as Circe, the fatal women of film noir are like their precursors in all the arts. The "beauteous" Homeric archetype is attired in haste, brings food and wine, enchants with her song, seduces with her smile, is a Goddess with deadly intent. From evening gowns to negligees, from berets to sun hats, in tight sweaters and high heels, the femme fatale is often literally and figuratively dressed to kill.

Opposite, J.W. Waterhouse's *Circe Invidiosa* (1892) and Rita Hayworth's iconic publicity pose for *Gilda* (1946). Below, lured onto the water, a hapless Alan Palmer (Arthur Kennedy) about to be shot with his own service pistol by his own wife Jane (Lizabeth Scott) in *Too Late for Tears* (1949).

Opposite, more deadly portents from women adrift: John William Waterhouse's 1888 depiction of *The Lady of Shalott* (top) and, wearing white robe and sunglasses, Gene Tierney as the treacherous Ellen Berent Harland in *Leave Her to Heaven* (1945).
Below, while a simple beret and a tight sweater may suffice for a B-movie Annie Laurie Starr, one of noir's deadliest females (Peggy Cummins, right, in 1949's *Gun Crazy* aka *Deadly is the Female*), Tierney's dark character is disarmingly elegant in a furred and bejeweled traveling outfit (bottom right) or upscale feathered hat, gloves, and darker fur (left).

Above, a bereted Cora (Lana Turner) cringes as her lover Frank (John Garfield) attacks her husband (Cecil Kellaway) in *The Postman Always Rings Twice* (1946).

Top, a wary Michèle Morgan as Nelly with Jean Gabin sports an authentic French beret in *Le Quai des Brumes* (1938).

Clockwise from top, the good, the bad, and the uncertain all sport berets: Lauren Bacall (with Humphrey Bogart) in *The Big Sleep* (1946); Dietrich in *Witness for the Prosecution* (1957); and Cleo More with Hugo Haas in *Strange Fascination* (1952).

Clockwise, the glamorous, Hedy Lamarr (below), and the pragmatic: Ingrid Bergman (opposite, top) in *Notorious* and Tierney in *Laura* (with Vincent Price).

This page: Linda Darnell as Stella in *Fallen Angel* (1945). Opposite, bottom, sun hats are functional, certainly so for Kathie Moffat (Jane Greer, left) tracked down in Mexico in *Out of the Past* (1947) and probably for Jenny Marsh (Patricia Knight) about to go on the run in *Shockproof* (1947). Top, the treacherous Kitty (Ava Gardner) opts for demure in *The Killers*, but the killer-socialite Helen Grayle (Claire Trevor) never dresses down in *Murder, My Sweet* (1944).

Motif - Furs, Feet, and Fetishes

Right, Neff (Fred MacMurrary) starts out admiring a “honey of an anklet” and ends up a double murderer in *Double Indemnity* (1945).

Below, Chris Cross (Edward G. Robinson) kneels to paint toenails for another Kitty (Joan Bennett) in *Scarlet Street* (1944). Page 44, Yvonne de Carlo handles her own case.

Opposite, Ida Lupino: as with Darnell on page 40, sometimes your feet just hurt.

CHECK HERE
LOCAL
STREET
EXIT

More Furs, Feet, Fetishes

One of the earliest noir fatal women, Mary Astor as Brigid O'Shaughnessy gives Bogart's Sam Spade a close look at her fox furs and coiffed tresses in 1941's *The Maltese Falcon.*

Opposite, Martin Rome (Richard Conte) slinks away as the violent masseuse Rose Given (Hope Emerson) is taken into custody in *Cry of the City* (1948).

Still More Furs

Donna Allen (Audrey Totter) cringes at the touch of Ray Milland as the demonic title character in *Alias Nick Beal* (1949).

Women wear the furs, and men cling to them. Sometimes as with doomed detective Paul Sheridan (Fred MacMurray), a man holds on to his femme fatale Lona (Kim Novak) and a gat, too, in *Pushover* (1954).
Opposite top, *Brute Force* (1947): Tom Lister (Whit Bissell) admires wife Cora (Ella Raines), as she self-admires in the mirror.

Opposite, from Alexis Smith (top left) in *Split Second* (1953) to Gloria Swanson (top right) as the grandiose Norma Desmond in *Sunset Boulevard* (1951), a quartet including Hedy Lamarr (bottom left) and Alida Valli (bottom, right) enveloped in fur.

This page, on the run: Kay Lawrence (Lizabeth Scott) with fugitive Frankie Madison (Burt Lancaster) in *I Walk Alone*. Below left, in *Where Danger Lives* (1950), a disturbed Margo (Faith Domergue) clings to Dr. Jeff Cameron (Robert Mitchum). Below, a determined Marie Windsor as Linda Belita in *Paradise Alley* 1962).

The Big Heat (1953): Debby Marsh (Gloria Grahame) opens up to Det. Dave Bannion (Glenn Ford).

Marlowe (Humphrey Bogart) rescues Vivian Rutledge (Lauren Bacall) in *The Big Sleep* (1946).

Ann Sheridan as the title figure in *Nora Prentiss* (1947) out clubbing with Dr. Talbot (Kent Smith).

Above. more men (in hats): Nick Magellan (Richard Conte) menaces Kathy Lupo (Anne Bancroft) in *New York Confidential* (1955).

A fez-wearing Doctor Omar (Victor Mature) attends to the luxuriating Poppy (Gene Tierney) in *Shanghai Gesture* (1941).

More *Double Indemnity*: Stanwyck's pose, costuming, and expression speak volumes about her personification of the conniving and murderous Phyllis Dietrichson.
Opposite, Joan Bennett takes a moment to admire her own figure in *The Secret Beyond the Door* (1947).
Bottom are Audrey Totter (right) and Lizabeth Scott (left).

Opposite, another quartet of sweater girls from Ann Savage (bottom right), counterclockwise to Cleo Moore, Lauren Bacall, and Gloria Grahame in *Human Desire* (1953).

Above, Ruth Roman in a pose that fully evokes the femme fatale, even holding a smouldering cigarette to suggest the character's own core of human desire.

In film noir, provocative poses often became posters, such as this languorous image of Ann Sheridan with boudoIr attire off the shoulder, manicured nails wrapped around a hand mirror, upswept hair reflected behind her that almost covers her left eye.

Opposite, even more provocative poses that became lobby cards: Marilyn Monroe in *Don't Bother to Knock* (1953, even the title is rife with implications) and, of course, seduction and firearms in *Gun Crazy*.

More Boudoir Attire

The Woman in the Window (1944): A nightmarish narrative in which dream girl Alice Reed (Joan Bennett) flirts with tough guy Heidt (Dan Duryea). Opposite, another nightmare: the tormented Leona Stepherson (Barbara Stanwyck) in *Sorry, Wrong Number* (1946).

Still sporting a hopeful smile at right, Marie Windsor is the prototype of older but still fatal woman over a decade from *The Killing* (1957) to *Paradise Alley* (1967).

A peignoir blanc is de rigueur for usually wholesome Veronica Lake on this page, where the only darkness is her shadow.

Opposite, peignoirs noirs suggest darker thoughts: clockwise from top right, a young Lana Turner peruses an alternate slipper choice; Faith Domergue clutches a dagger; but Gloria Grahame flashes nothing more menacing than a pout in *The Big Heat.*

Criminals, Killers, and Sociopaths

The fatal men of film noir have no monopoly on how and why they come to kill. Like Brigid O'Shaughnessy or Phyllis Dietrichson, the female protoypes evince much the same reasons, with the usual lust, greed, and envy at the head of the list. For a few, an inner darkness drives them to a full-blown sociopathy that makes the pistol-packing Annie Laurie Starr seem normal in comparison.

In *Angel Face* (1953) neither ambulance driver Frank Jessup (Robert Mitchum, who often attracts fatal women) nor the viewer suspect—despite the telling shadow over his face and the blank look on hers—that young heiress Diane Tremayne (Jean Simmons) is other than the innocent she apprears to be.

Another sociopath: like a figure from Greek myth, the coldly determined and dual-named Gabrielle/Lily Carver (Gaby Rodgers) cannot help herself. She compulsively opens the "great whatsit" in *Kiss Me Deadly* (1955) and discovers a box of pure phlogiston.

TERRY

Where Danger Lives: Faith Domergue as the desperate and disturbed Margo. As her hand claws at the arm of her injured lover Jeff Cameron (Robert Mitchum, perhaps the most frequent target of fatal women in all of film noir), the play of light across her unnaturally placid gaze externalizes her inner state.

Previous page, left, concealing a cold-blooded sociopathy is often about performance, Gene Tierney as Helen feigns real emotion for the benefit of husband Richard (Cornel WIlde) in *Leave Her to Heaven*. Helen is much more composed pouring out a dose of poison (at the bottom of the next page).

Previous right, Olivia de Havilland both Terry and Ruth Collins: as the poster above says, "Twins, one who loves... and one who loves to kill!" Killer Terry can go from a placid expression (previous right top) to full mania (bottom), with sidelight on her face to underscore visually her schizophrenic mind.

Mildred Pierce (1944): Ann Blyth and the dissociative stare of Velda, the avaricious and deadly teenage daughter of Joan Crawford's long-suffering title character.

Motif - Women with Guns

Sometimes scared...sometimes not. At times glamourous but often hard-bitten and deadly. With fingers on the trigger, clockwise from top left: Barbara Payton (*Kiss Tomorrow Goodbye*). Alexis Smith (*Undercover Girl*), Barbara Hayden (*Crimson Kimono*), and Martha Vickers (*The Burglar*).

A Woman's Secret (1949): Gloria Grahame in the boudoir with a Luger. Opposite, the haughty Gilda (Rita Hayworth) with her .32 automatic in *Lady from Shanghai*.

The deadly female Annie Laurie Starr (Peggy Cummins), a side-show performer (inset on page 75) turned stick-up artist in *Gun Crazy*.

PAYROL

Coca-Cola
Coca-Cola

More Gun Craziness

Bart Tare (John Dall) restrains the enraged Annie, who can also look the ingenue (inset) but epitomize fatal women who are “thrill crazy, kill crazy, gun crazy.”

Out of the Past: a remarkably unconcerned Kathie Moffat (Jane Greer) watches and waits as the figures seen only in shadow fight. Opposite, a posed partial doppelganger of a determined Joan Crawford as Mildred Pierce. Note the clenched left hand.

Ingenues: opposite page, Gaby Rodgers as Lily Carver in *Kiss Me Deadly*. Below, a young Rita Hayworth with a revolver. Above, Carmen (Martha Vickers) fingers an automatic in *The Big Sleep.*

Underworld and Gangster Romances

GUN MOLLS

MAGAZINE

Opposite, *Gun Molls Magazine*: Jane from Hell's Kitchen packs two pistols. The pulp fiction of the 1920s and '30s and the women of the gangster genre anticipate the Women with Guns in film noir.

Above, prototype of the gun-toting fatal woman: Clara Bow in 1928's *Ladies of the Mob.* Two decades later Betty Lou Gerson, at right, is every bit as hard-bitten and dangling a coffin nail from her sneering lips in *The Red Menace* (1949).

Variations on a Theme: A Woman behind a Man with a Gun

Noir icon/moll Barbara Payton cowers behind her criminal companions: Lloyd Bridges (opposite in *Trapped* (1949) and James Cagney (below) in *Kiss Tomorrow Goodbye.*

Variations on a Theme: A Woman next to a Man with a Gun

In *Pushover* Kim Novak mirrors Payton's apprehension. Opposite top, Veronica Lake seems less concerned when posed with Alan Ladd and his automatic in *Blue Dahlia.* Opposite bottom, perhaps the larger firearm inspires Helen Walker's smiling confidence when she stands behind Ladd in *Lucky Jordan*.

The Big Heat: only Gloria Grahame's B-girl/moll Debby is confident enough to pose in front of the man with the gun (Glenn Ford). While the camera placement and expression of Mona Stevens (Lizabeth Scott) in a posed shot for *Pitfall* are both determined and menacing, MacDonald (Raymond Burr) controls his apprehension.

Lured (1947): Sandra Carpenter (Lucille Ball) calmly faces off against Robert Fleming (George Sanders).

Spin a Dark Web (1960): Faith Domergue as Bella closes her eyes before firing.

Laura: Gene Tierney holds a shotgun with uncertainty.

Stolen Face (1952): Dr. Philip Ritter (Paul Henreid) and Alice Brent (Lizabeth Scott) share a toast at a local pub.

At the Bar

Sometimes you drink angry and alone, as with Audrey Totter's Donna Allen in *Alias Nick Beal* (1949). Most often it's tête-à-tête with the protagonist, such as Lenore Brent (Jane Russell) and Dan Milner (Robert Mitchum) in *His Kind of Woman* (1951), below.

Two Anne Brancroft barflies: above, with Richard Widmark in *Don't Bother to Knock* and, below, raising a glass with Aldo Ray in *Nightfall* (1957).

More uncertain encounters: Ella Raines as Deborah and George Sanders as the title character in *The Strange Affair of Uncle Harry* (1945).

Novak and MacMurray as the doomed lovers in *Pushover.*

Still Others at the Bar: above, alcoholic writer Dixon Steele (Humphrey Bogart) fixated on Laurel Gray (Gloria Grahame) in *In A Lonely Place* (1950).Opposite, top to bottom, *Woman on the Run* (1950), a bar can also be a place to ask questions: bartender Sullivan (Syd Sailor) watches as blond patron (Joan Fulton) talks to reporter Dan Legget (Dennis O'Keefe) and Eleanor Johnson (Ann Sheridan) about her missing husband. *Phantom Lady* (1944): Faye Helm as the title character has a chance encounter with Scott Henderson (Alan Curtis). Uncle Charlie (Joseph Cotten) takes his namesake and underaged niece (Teresa Wright) to a local joint in *Shadow of a Doubt* (1943). Richard Egan's bartender Matt Bannister is more sociable as he pours one for Billie Nash (Beverly Michaels) in *Wicked Woman* (1953).

More At the Bar

Clockwise from opposite page top, disinherited Arnold Waring (Dan Duryea) and murder witness Nicki Collins (Deanna Durbin) are interrupted by Mr. Sanders (George Coulouris), a circus manager in clown costume in *Lady on a Train* (1945). Club photographer Lila Crane (Cleo Moore) with reporter Russ Bassett (Richard Crenna) in *Over-exposed* (1956). Carol "Kansas" Richman (Ella Raines) is determined to get the truth from a witness-bartender (Andrew Tombes) in *Phantom Lady*. Frank and Diane early in their twisted coutrtship in *Angel Face.*

Motif - A Toast

Notorious (1946): neither the smile of Alicia Huberman (Ingrid Bergman) nor the scowl of Devlin (Cary Grant) prompts a toast, unlike the instances where men might be sociopaths in *The House on Telegraph Hill* (1951) with Valentina Cortese and Richard Basehart or *Secret Beyond the Door* (1947) with Michael Redgrave and Joan Bennett.

Pitfall: John Forbes (Dick Powell) and Mona Stevens (Lizabeth Scott) toast the beginning of their adulterous affair.

Out of the Past: A toast to what will become one of film noir's most treacherous liaisons, Jane Greer's fatal woman holds her cigarette to the side above a purse with her oversized initials. Mitchum's Jeff Markham only has eyes for her.

Eating and drinking at home: secretary Kathleen (Lucille Ball) is dismayed to see her boss P.I. Bradford Galt (Mark Stevens) pour an impromptu mixed drink In *The Dark Corner* (1946).

Opposite, a fatal woman spoils dessert: Andrea King as the conniving Marjorie confronts Robert Montgomery as Lucky Gagin and Wanda Hendrix as Pila in *Ride the Pink Horse*.

Eating and drinking at the kitchen table can be glum for Marko (Hugo Haas) and Peggy (Cleo Moore) in *Bait* (1953).

New York Confidential (1955): Anne Bancroft has some food with her drink in the company of Nick Magellan (Richard Conte).

Criss Cross (1949): Steve Thompson (Burt Lancaster) prepares food and contemplates his relationship to ex-wife Anna (Yvonne De Carlo). Opposite, Bogart's Rip Murdock warily regards the often deadly Lizabeth Scott as Dusty in *Dead Reckoning* (1947).

Scarlet Street (1945): Kitty (Joan Bennett) eats, drinks, smokes and casts an anxious look at boyfriend/ pimp Johnny Prince (Dan Duryea). She knows his thinking can bring trouble.

Neither nicotine nor alcohol seems to alleviate the ennui for Joan Crawford as Helen Wright in *Humoresque* (1946).

Smoking

As with the classic pose from *Gilda* on page 32, an essential element in the pose of a fatal woman is often the curling wisp of smoke from the cigarette, like the one held by Anne Francis in her tight sweater or a pouting, beret-wearing Ingrid Bergman from *Arch of Triumph* (1948) on the next page.

While Bergman's hard-bitten Joan Madou lets the cigarette dangle from her lips, in a more typical pose, opposite, Hedy Lamarr makes the coffin nail a glamorous accessory.

Joan Bennett's "model"/call girl Kitty, opposite in *Scarlet Street,* is much deadlier than Ida Lupino's torch singing Petey Brown in *The Man I Love* (1947); yet the matching come-hither poses with or without the curling smoke identify them both as women to beware of. Compare with Ava Gardner on page 6.

Next two pages, an array of female smokers (clockwise across both pages): Mary Astor, Lizabeth Scott, Jane Greer, Valentina Cortese, Ann Sheridan, Cleo Moore, and Ann Savage.

Motif - Light Me

The sexual context in the act of lighting someone else's cigarette was established long before the noir movement. The expression on the face of Jack Palance as Lester Blaine may explain why Gloria Grahame's Irene is lighting her own in *Sudden Fear* (1952).

The posed expression of Ella Raines, opposite, as defiant as it may be alluring.

Motif - Light Me

Lighting another's cigarette is a fleeting yet somewhat intimate act with a highly volatile contact point. In *The Woman in the Window*, Professor Richard Wanley (Edward G. Robinson) leans in slightly but the distance between him and Alice Reed (Joan Bennett) is maintained, even underscored by her gloved hand and cigarette holder.

Motif - Light Me

B-girl Myrna Bowers (Cleo Moore) adds a physical connection, as she lifts the hand of rogue cop Jim Wilson (Robert Ryan) in *On Dangerous Ground* (1951),

Below, the conniving Helen Grayle (Claire Trevor) wraps all her fingers around the hand of private dick Philip Marlowe (Dick Powell) in *Murder, My Sweet* (1944).

Secretary Carol "Kansas" Richman (Ella Raines) tries to reassure her imprisoned boss Scott Henderson (Alan Curtis) with a shared smoke in *Phantom Lady.* Below, Evelyn (Faith Domergue) uses a look and a lit match to communicate her desire to Glenn Harris (Rick Jason) in *This Is My Love* (1954).

The Three (or Four) Faces of Lizabeth Scott: above, the avaricious Jane Palmer accepts a light from the clearly wary Don Blanchard (Don DeFore) in *Too Late for Tears.* Opposite top, an ex-con trying to go straight, Toni Marachek lets a conflicted Sam Masterson (Van Heflin) "match" her in *The Strange Love of Martha Ivers* (1946). Bottom, Mona Stevens unenthusiastically accepts a light from ex-cop J.B. MacDonald (Raymond Burr), who will soon become her stalker in *Pitfall.* Left and below, Coral "Dusty" Chandler is distracted from her unhappy reverie by a match profferred by "Rip" Murdock (Humphrey Bogart) in *Dead Reckoning.*

Most men lean over including Kent Smith, opposite top, with Ann Sheridan in *Nora Prentiss*, Charles Coburn with Helen Walker in *Impact* (1949), and Gary Merrill with Jan Sterling in *The Human Jungle* (1954); but there is no bending for the diffident Clifton Webb with Arlene Dahl in *A Woman's World* (1954).

The Postman Always Rings Twice (1946): as their faces reflect, every interaction is fraught with peril for Frank Chambers (John Garfield) and Cora Smith (Lana Turner), because they are enmeshed in a web of adultery, murder, and betrayal.

Phantom Lady: Carol Richman does a lot more than just take dictation when she visits her boss in prison.

Models and Secretaries

After accepting work as a live-in personal secretray Julia Ross (Nina Foch, above) is drugged and “gaslighted” by Ralph Hughes (George Macready), the son of her employer, in *My Name is Julia Ross* (1945).

If there is a prototypical film noir secretary it is Lucille Ball as Kathleen Stewart, here politely fielding questions from Detective Lt. Frank Reeves (Reed Hadley) about her boss, private investigator Bradford Galt.

The Inner Circle (1946): if secretary Gerry Travis (Mala Powers) seems conflicted, it may because she framed her boss P.I. Johnny Strange (Warren Douglas, left), facing Det. Lt. Webb (William Frawley), to protect her sister. Below, secretary/con woman Bridget Kelly (Yvonne De Carlo) has planted the wallet she stole from Leonard Wilson (Victor Jory) on Clementi Sabourin (George Sanders), who stares at her derisively in *Death of a Scoundrel* (1954).

Above, *Manhandled* (1949): private secretary Merl Kramer (Dorothy Lamour) betrays a secret of her psychiatrist boss to her treacherous boyfriend, P.I. Karl Benson (Dan Duryea, left), whose frame job arouses the suspicion of Det. Lt. Bill Dawson (Art Smith).

Right, Ella Raines as the intensely loyal Carol "Kansas" Richman ponders her next investigative option in *Phantom Lady.*

JUNE

Left, Velda Wickman (Maxine Cooper) is more than just a secretary to shady P.I. Mike Hammer (Ralph Meeker) in *Kiss Me Deadly*. Above, *Pillow of Death* (1945): Donna Kincaid (Brenda Joyce) is more than a secretary to attorney Wayne Fletcher (Lon Chaney, Jr.) who is greatly disturbed by visions of his murdered wife. Right, Mona Stevens (Lizabeth Scott) models a gown for insurance investigator and stalker J.B. MacDonald (Raymond Burr) in *Pitfall.*

Model or Call Girl?
Joan Bennett's Kitty tells Edward G. Robinson's Chris Cross that she's a model but wears an outfit and strikes a pose more appropriate to her actual occupation.

There is no question about what Candy (Jean Peters) does in *Pickup on South Street* (1953). She dresses the part; but the cops flanking her want to know if she is also a Commie spy.

Call Girl or Show Girl?

Jan Sterling's Mary Abbott walks the line standing defiantly between two cops or, opposite, facing down her fellow performers in *The Human Jungle.*

The occupation of Rica (Valentina Cortese) is clear, but she may be having second thoughts about setting up angry trucker Nick Garcos (Richard Conte) in *Thieves' Highway* (1949).

Beyond a Reasonable Doubt (1956): Det. Kennedy (Edward Binns) questions dancers Dolly Moore (Barbara Nichols, left) and Terry Larue (Robin Raymond).

Just a Showgirl?

Opposite, Det. Leonard Diamond (Cornel Wilde) visits dancer girlfriend Rita (Helene Stanton) in *The Big Combo* (1955)

Right, ambitious singer Netta Longdon (Linda Darnell) as innocent as she appears in *Hangover Square* (1945)?

Motif - Torch Singing

A diffident (and doomed) Fran Ledue Page (Gloria Grahame) prepares to belt out a lament in *Song of the Thin Man* (1947).

Opposite, cynical and sultry Julie Benson (Jane Russell) drops anchor in the titled locale *Macao* (1952) for at least a couple of sets with the local players.

Next page, in another exotic locale off the coast of Central America,the expression of café singer Elizabeth Hintten (Ava Gardner) may reflect her growing suspicions about her expatriate husband in *The Bribe* (1949).

Selling the Song

Madi Comfort croons some blue notes (as P.I. Mike Hammer drowns his sorrows off-screen) and holds the microphone in a manner that alarmed censors around the country in *Kiss Me Deadly.* Below, title character Gilda Farrell (Rita Hayworth) famously puts her entire body into a rendition of "Put the Blame on Mame."

The club's spotlight is full on Coral "Dusty" Chandler (Lizabeth Scott) as she uses a torch song to sell Capt. "Rip" Murdock (Humphrey Bogart) on her innocence in *Dead Reckoning*.

Sometimes you tickle your own ivories as with Marie Windsor at left or Ida Lupino (opposite as Lily Stevens in 1948's *Roadhouse*). Other times a piano helps you, as with Hoagy Carmichael's Cricket with Lauren Bacall's Marie "Slim" Browning in *To Have and Have Not* (1944).

Part Two: Roll Call

The A List

> You know you don't have to act with me. You don't have to say anything, and you don't have to do anything. Oh, maybe just whistle. You know how to whistle, don't you? You just put your lips together and... blow.
>
> *To Have and Have Not*

Lauren Bacall

Much like the proto-femme fatale Clara Bow, as a teenager Lauren Bacall had "It." In her roles opposite husband Humphrey Bogart, particularly in *To Have and Have Not* and *The Big Sleep*, she tends to dominate the frame, even shadow Bogart (below and see also page 37).

Bacall's self-confident posture and smoky voice reinforced the effortless impact of her glances, whether lighting her man's smoke, above in *To Have and Have Not*, or a more pointed disapproval aimed at the gun held by Luis Denard (Charles Boyer) in *Confidential Agent* (1945) or the perspiring Marlowe in *The Big Sleep*.

Joan Bennett

Joan Bennett is one of the key femme fatales of the noir classic period. Her portrayals of avaricious predators in Fritz Lang's *Scarlet Street* [see pages 42, 108, 114, and 138] and *The Woman in the Window* (opposite bottom, and pages 58 and 120) were unparalleled in their disdain for their patriarchal, bourgeois victims, both played by Edward G. Robinson, eschewing any gangster persona to great effect. In *The Woman on the Beach* (1947) Bennett's affair almost results in the death of both her husband and lover.

This page as Cella Lamphere in *The Secret Beyond the Door* [see also 53 and 99].

Opposite top, as victim of chance Lucia Harper in *The Reckless Moment* (1949).

Ingrid Bergman

Ingrid Bergman only took on the role of a fatal woman a few times in her checkered career in Hollywood, most notably in the Hitchcock films *Notorious* with Cary Grant [see page 98] and *Under Capricorn* (1949, with Joseph Cotten). After *Spellbound*, her first film with him in 1945, Hitchcock was able to tap into the dark sexuality of Bergman's character, while most of the other films in her career tended to emphasize her wholesomeness and Nordic spiritual beauty [see also pages 39 and 112].

Below, an anxious Bergman as Alicia suspects that the ministrations of her husband Alexander Sebastian (Claude Rains) and mother-in-law (Leopoldine Konstantin) are not meant to cure her ailment. Opposite, realizing what has been done to her, the tormented, knife-wielding Paula contemplates revenge on her scheming husband Gregory Anton (Claude Boyer) in *Gaslight* (1944).

Peggy Cummins

Peggy Cummins will always be remembered for her landmark role as Annie Laurie Starr in Joseph H. Lewis' *Gun Crazy* (written under a pseudonym by blacklisted writer Dalton Trumbo). Her unadulterated sexuality combined with a self-destructive taste for violence relentlessly drives the trajectory of the movie and the destiny of her male lover Bart Tare (John Dall), even when he thinks he's at the wheel (below).

Before Annie Laurie, Cummins was Belle/Rose in *Moss Rose* (1947, opposite), a chorus girl who blackmails the upper class male protagonist (Victor Mature) so that she can escape the poverty and seediness of her present life [see also pages 35 and 72-75].

Arlene Dahl

In 1956 Arlene Dahl crafted two noteworthy noir performances. In *Wicked As They Come* (below, with Philip Carey as Tim O'Bannion) Dahl plays Kathy, a poor girl from the slums, a victim of gang rape, who takes her revenge by using man after man to raise her social status as well as cause them to feel a little of the pain she suffered. In Allan Dwan's *Slightly Scarlet* she is the sexually charged, morally challenged Dorothy, who is the evil half of a pair of scarlet-tressed sisters with Rhonda Fleming (left, opposite). [See also page 127.]

Dorothy Dandridge

Dorothy Dandridge was the first African American actress to reach the A-list of stars in Hollywood. She was nominated for two major awards (an Oscar and a Golden Globe) for her performances in *Carmen Jones* (1954), opposite Harry Belafonte, and *Porgy and Bess* (1959) opposite Sidney Poitier, both directed by noir veteran Otto Preminger. *Carmen Jones* was updated to modern day but basically followed the same story of the free-spirited Carmen as created by Bizet for his 19th-century opera. George Gershwin's *Porgy and Bess* again utilized Dandridge's singing and acting skills to portray the psychologically and emotionally turbulent object of Porgy's obsession.

Below, a carnal moment with Belafonte in *Carmen Jones.* Opposite, singing the blues as Norma Sherman in the noir television series *Cain's Hundred* (1962).

Linda Darnell

Linda Darnell projected a strength of will which matched the macho personas of her antagonists like Dana Andrews in *Fallen Angel* (below, see also page 40) or Cornel Wilde in *Forever Amber*. Even as the angry widow Edie Johnson in *No Way Out* (1950, opposite botton), she outwits her racist brother-in-law. And when her victim was a conflicted, sensitive composer like Laird Cregar in *Hangover Square* (opposite, see also page 143), the game was over at first glance.

Bette Davis

Although known for her more mainstream "award-worthy" roles as in *Now Voyager* or *All About Eve,* Bette Davis ventured into the area of noir several times, most notably in *The Letter* (1940) and *Beyond the Forest* (1949). In *The Letter*, based on Somerset Maugham's story, Davis plays the wife of a cuckolded rubber plantation owner in Malaya who not only cheats on her husband (Herbert Marshall) but also murders her recalcitrant lover. She then manipulates her lawyer, who manages to obtain an acquittal. The steamy atmosphere of Malaya enhances the noir atmospherics. In *Beyond the Forest* Davis plays Rosa Moline, a sultry protagonist who is stifled by small town life and her milquetoast husband (Joseph Cotten), leading her to find adventure in romantic entanglements which ultimately bring about disaster. Below, in white fur and hood Davis as tormented pianist Christine Radcliffe shoots her former lover conductor Alexander Hollenius (Claude Rains) in *Deception* (1946).

Rosa Moline in a pose that reflects her frustration at being trapped in an unglamourous life, even as the flames in the background externalize her inner emotions.

The Letter: In one of the most sensational opening sequences in early film noir, Davis as Leslie Crosbie calmly guns down a man she claims tried to assault her. She follows him out of the house and pulls the trigger until her smoking revolver has no live rounds remaining.

Faith Domergue

Faith Domergue, now most famous as magnate Howard Hughes' teenage protégé (she appears as a character in Martin Scorsese's *The Aviator*), had a remarkable debut performance as the fiery, violent Colomba (opposite and page 60) in the film maudit *Vendetta* (released in 1950 after four years in production). Then she portrayed the clinging, psychotic Margo in *Where Danger Lives* (below and also pages 49 and 66) opposite the prototypical noir "chump," Robert Mitchum. After Hughes, Domergue worked in Westerns and sci-fi but also made two British noir films: *Soho Incident* (1956, aka *Spin a Dark Web,* see page 88) and *Man in the Shadow* (1958, aka *Violent Stranger*). [See also page 123.]

Even as Mitchum's Dr. Jeff Cameron grabs Margo's wrist, the curl of her fingers and her expression confirm that she has already sunk her claws into him.

Ava Gardner

Ava Gardner's signature noir femme fatale role is in Robert Siodmak's *The Killers*, opposite noir icon Burt Lancaster. As Kitty, Gardner uses her languorous style (as in the pose in the hide-out on these pages) and whisky voice to run circles around Lancaster's "Swede," leaving him depleted and ready to accept death in the opening of the film. Almost a decade later Gardner brings to life the character of the sensual, independent Maria Vargas in director-writer Joseph Mankiewicz's tale of Hollywood corruption, *The Barefoot Contessa* (1954), exotically costumed in the inset at right. While various powerful men try to control Maria, she remains faithful to her own spirit, no matter the effect on these men.

The posed shot for *The Killers* underscores Kitty as a faux naif seductress (see also pages 6 and 40). Opposite, *The Bribe*, where Gardner assumes very different postures vis-à-vis her ne'er-do-well husband "Tug" (John Hodiak, top) and her new love interest, federal agent Rigby (Robert Taylor). [See also page 146.]

Gloria Grahame

Gloria Grahame starred in three of the key noir films of the 1950s: *In A Lonely Place* (see page 95), *The Big Heat*, and *Human Desire*. Grahame's slight lisp and blond locks (as coded in Hollywood films, see the posed shot on the opposite page) gave her a vulnerability, which mitigated some of the aggressiveness of the traditional femme fatale. In *Human Desire*, Fritz Lang's loose adaptation of Emile Zola's *La Bête Humaine*, she is a pouting victim as much as conniver (see page 55), brutalized by her jealous husband Carl (Broderick Crawford). In *The Big Heat*, her disfigured moll Debby Marsh [see page 50] acts partly for revenge and partly for redemption in the eyes of callous detective Dave Bannion (Glenn Ford), who uses her without bothering to make excuses. [See also pages 61, 70 (*One Woman's Story*), 86, 118 (*Sudden Fear*), and 144 (*Song of the Thin Man*).]

Below, cigarette in hand Grahame's Vicky Buckley checks outside her window while her lover Jeff Warren (also Glenn Ford) peeks more furtively from behind a curtain. On pages 180-181 *The Big Heat*: a still beautiful Debby poses in front of a mirror in the arms of her mobster boyfriend Vince Stone (Lee Marvin), who will later throw scalding coffee in her face.

Jane Greer

Jane Greer had a relatively short career as a fatal woman. In the minor film *The Company She Keeps* (1951, see below), she portrays Diane Stuart, an ex-convict who keeps wandering astray despite the help offered by Joan Wilburn (Lizabeth Scott), the ostensible "good girl" of the piece.

Greer's Pantheon status relies almost entirely on the landmark *Out of the Past*. As the unrelentingly avaricious Kathie Moffat (see also pages 41, 76, 101-103, and 117), she set a pattern for countless femme fatales to follow, as much as Barbara Stanwyck or Lana Turner did in their respective key noir films *Double Indemnity* and *The Postman Always Rings Twice*.

Opposite, in 1953, Greer reteamed with Robert Mitchum in Mexico for Don Siegel's noir-style semi-spoof *The Big Steal.*

Below, with Lizabeth Scott in *The Company She Keeps.* On pages 184-185, as the treacherous, fur-clad Kathie, compelled to make a phone call by gunsel Joe Stefanos (Paul Valentine) in *Out of the Past*.

Rita Hayworth

While not often cast as a Latina, Rita Hayworth (born Margarita Cansino, see page 78) reached iconic status with *Gilda*. The title character overcomes patriarchal restraints in a manner akin to a feminist warrior: sexually liberated, smart, the equal of any man, even the most powerful, who attempt to fence her in. Gilda refuses to submit to their control. Because of *Gilda*'s success, Hayworth was locked into that image, on and off screen, for the next decade. The rueful quote attributed to her says it all: "They go to bed with Gilda; they wake up with me." Director and then husband Orson Welles reinvented her femme fatale persona in his baroque noir *The Lady from Shanghai*. Six years after *Gilda*, she reteamed with Glenn Ford in the lackluster Caribbean noir *Affair in Trinidad* (1952, below). [See also pages 32 and 147.]

Gilda: playboy Johnny Farrell (Glenn Ford) seems more interested in his sports car and his cigarette than in the glamourous Gilda.

The Lady from Shanghai: the fun-house mirrors sequence with Hayworth as Elsa Bannister and Orson Welles as Michael O'Hara. (See also page 71.)

Jennifer Jones

Jennifer Jones' career over two decades included many "prestige" films from *The Song of Bernadette* (1943) to Vincente Minnelli's *Madame Bovary* (1949), De Sica's *Stazione Termini* (1953), and an adaptation of F. Scott Fitzgerald's *Tender Is the Night* (1962). Her two "trashier" films stand as pure noir fatal woman: *Duel in the Sun* (1946) and *Ruby Gentry* (1953). Jones' portrayal of the mixed-race Pearl defies Western stereotype. Unwilling to submit to the predatory desires of any man, she forms a Wagnerian love/hate relationship with the amoral Lewt (Gregory Peck) that results in as self-destructive a couple as any in traditional film noir. *Ruby Gentry* revisits the same motifs and like *Duel in the Sun* ends with another gunfight driven by *amour fou* between Ruby, Boake (Charlton Heston), and her Bible-thumping brother (James Anderson).

Below, Jones as Ruby Gentry lights a cigarette for Boake Tackman (Charlton Heston).

Opposite, Jones as Pearl Chavez with Gregory Peck as Lewt McCanles in *Duel in the Sun.*

Hedy Lamarr

Hedy Lamarr's credentials as a fatal woman had already been established by the time she fled Nazi Europe in 1937. Her Czech film *Ecstasy* (1933) created a worldwide scandal, as it featured nude scenes of Lamarr swimming. More importantly, she portrayed a sexually liberated protagonist who rejects her asexual husband for a passionate young lover. Her performance as the native seductress ("I am Tondelayo.") in *White Cargo* (1942) opposite Walter Pidgeon solidified her exotic position in Hollywood. Not satisfied with just being a hired worker Lamarr (who was also an inventor), formed her own company and produced the low-budget potboiler *The Strange Woman* directed by Edgar G. Ulmer. She appeared in another period noir in the *Gaslight* vein, *Experiment Perilous* (1944, directed by Jacques Tourneur), and, as well, in her contemporary production *Dishonored Lady* (1947) and *A Lady with a Passport* (1950, directed by Joseph H. Lewis).

Below, *Dishonored Lady*: Lamarr as fashion editor Madeleine Damien having a bite with Dennis O'Keefe as David Cousins. Opposite top, as Jenny Hager with George Sanders as John Evered and Hillary Brooke as Meg Saladine, the best friend Jenny betrays in *The Stange Woman.* Bottom, *Experiment Perilous*, as Allida Bederaux with George Brent as Dr. Huntington Bailey and Paul Lukas as her controlling husband Nick.

titled figure lady with a passport, on a raft in the Everglades between the scarred, Cuban-based smuggler Palinov (Macready) and INS Agent Frank Westlake (James Craig).

Ida Lupino

British-born actor (and later director) Ida Lupino stepped into the role of a fatal woman only a few times. The first was in *They Drive by Night* (1940) as the mentally unstable Lana who kills her husband in order to marry her object of obsession, Joe (George Raft), and then accuses Joe of the murder when he refuses to marry her. Other noir figures in her films at Warner Bros. ranged from youthful moll opposite Bogart in *High Sierra* (1941) to the blues singer in *The Man I Love* (see also page 115). At Fox she portrayed another singer with blond bangs in *Roadhouse* (see also page 151) and at Universal *Woman in Hiding* (1949). Later in her career after she had directed such noir films as *The Bigamist* and *The Hitch-Hiker* (both 1953), she produced and starred in the Don Siegel film *Private Hell 36* (1954) as the greedy torch singer who leads a cop (played by her then husband Howard Duff) astray. Lupino concluded her career as a film noir performer with *The Big Knife* (1955) for Robert Aldrich and *While the City Sleeps* (1956) for Fritz Lang.

At Warners: Lupino as Lana Carlsen with Ann Sheridan as Cassie Hartley and George Raft as Joe Fabrini in *They Drive by Night*. Opposite, with Bruce Bennett as San Thomas in *The Man I Love.*

Lupino as the bruised moll Marie with Bogart as "Mad Dog" Roy Earle in *High Sierra*.

The many noir faces of Lupino over more than fifteen years: *Moontide* (1942) with Jean Gabin; below, *Woman in Hiding* with Howard Duff; opposite top, *Roadhouse* with Richard Widmark; and bottom, *Private Hell 36* with Steve Cochran.

More noir faces: as the blind Mary Malden in *On Dangerous Ground*; opposite top, actor and director lighting her own cigarette as Phyllis Martin with Edmond O'Brien in *The Bigamist*; bottom, fighting husband Charlie Castle (Jack Palance) in *The Big Knife.*

Marilyn Monroe

Although Marilyn Monroe may be best remembered for her light comic roles, she was also capable of playing the alluring yet psychologically damaged fatal lady who could turn on the "little girl magic" at the drop of a hat. Her debut was as the corrupt lawyer's concupiscent young mistress in John Huston's *The Asphalt Jungle* (1950).

In *Don't Bother to Knock* (see page 57), she is suicidal, homicidal, and delusional but manipulative enough to bamboozle the men in the piece. In *Niagara* (1953, opposite top) Monroe is at once deceptive and seductive, this time cuckolding her older husband (Joseph Cotten) right under his nose and then planning his murder.

Fritz Lang's *Clash by Night* (1952): Monroe appears in another supporting role as the youthful Peggy. Opposite, as the concupiscent Angela Phinlay who will soon recant her alibi under pressure from Det. Andrews (Don Haggerty) in *The Asphalt Jungle*.

Cleo Moore

Cleo Moore distilled her version of the fatal woman in collaboration with low-budget émigré director Hugo Haas. In many ways the couple were a low-rent version of Dietrich and von Sternberg in their personal lives as well as in their films. Moore played a series of aggressive, sexually liberated females who could be ruthless in pursuit of their desires. Although the films were often ignored, they are now considered cult classics: *Strange Fascination* (see page 37), *One Girl's Confession* (1953), *Thy Neighbor's Wife* (1953), *Bait* (see page 105), *The Other Woman* (1954), *Hold Back Tomorrow* (1955), and *Hit and Run* (1957). While admittedly much less polished, these films share many of the same themes, motifs, and tropes as the Dietrich/von Sternberg series in the 1930s. [See also pages 54, 97, 117, and 122).

Riding the train with Hugo Haas in *Bait*.
Opposite, serving drinks for the barkeep (Arthur Marshall) in *One Girl's Confession.*

GIN
4/5 QUART
DUBLIN
A BLEND OF

About to be whipped in *Thy Neighbor's Wife*.

Below, sampling jail food with John Agar as Ray Brighton in *Bait*.

Mary Murphy

Mary Murphy delivers two notable performances as a femme fatale, the first in the UK for the blacklisted American director Joseph Losey, *Intimate Stranger* (aka *Finger of Guilt*, 1956). A director (Richard Basehart) is unjustly accused (echoes of the blacklist are obvious) by an actress (Murphy) of having an affair with her and then dumping her. Returning for some payback, Murphy radiates the dangerous sensuality that later informed her tour de force performance as the unrepentant fatal woman in Phil Karlson's *Hell's Island* (1955). The use of Technicolor In *Hell's Island* heightens Murphy's "allure" from her red lips and blond hair to her zebra-striped bikini. A side note: the movie's poster with Murphy posed in a diaphanous peignoir while holding a revolver (right) was used as an example of "degenerate" Hollywood during the 1950s Kefauver Congressional Hearings. Also in 1955 Murphy was petite enough to play the teenage daughter in *The Desperate Hours* and again three years later as a larcenous teen runaway in the beat generation noir *Live Fast, Die Young* (1958).

Above, Murphy as Kim Winters packs to leave home as her father (Gordon Jones) watches in *Live Fast, Die Young.*

Right, posed with a half smile and a Luger in *Intimate Stranger.*

Opposite, as Janet Martin fighting off John Payne as Mike Cormack in *Hell's Island.*

Kim Novak

Kim Novak's femme fatale debut in *Pushover* consciously alluded to *Double Indemnity* with the casting of Fred MacMurray as a rogue cop. Although Novak's Lona McLane is a much more sympathetic figure than Stanwyck's Phyllis Dietrichson, she also leads a "chump" MacMurray character to his destruction (see also pages 47, 85, and 93).

Much more complex is the role of Judy/Madeleine in Hitchcock's *Vertigo* (1958), where Novak's dual characters again draw an ex-cop/investigator through a psychological maze. Her dual characters have control of the narrative, as they only merge after an ironic reveal to the viewer but not to the ex-cop (James Stewart) of her machinations. Novak also appeared as the female member of a robbery crew in Phil Karlson's noir caper movie *Five Against the House* (1955). Her final performance was in the neo-noir *Liebestraum* (1991).

Fatal-woman mirror shots: below as Lona McLane with Fred MacMurray as Det. Paul Sheridan in *Pushover.* Opposite bottom, as Judy Barton with James Stewart as the obsessed Scottie Ferguson in *Vertigo.*

As Kaye Greylek crooning in Vegas in *Five Against the House.*

Lizabeth Scott

Lizabeth Scott with her dusky voice and direct manner was perfect for a fatal woman. In fact she played two of the most brutal fatal ladies in the noir canon. In both *Dead Reckoning* (see also pages 106, 116, 124 and 148-149) and *Too Late for Tears* (see also pages 33 and 124), she expressed very few qualms about manipulating and even murdering the men in her life.

On screen Scott held her own against formidable noir males such as Humphrey Bogart and Dan Duryea. She also held her own in several pictures with Burt Lancaster, Kirk Douglas, Robert Mitchum, and Charlton Heston: *I Walk Alone* (see also page 49), *The Strange Love of Martha Ivers* (see also page 125), *Desert Fury* (1947, see also pages 2-3), *Dark City* (1950), *The Racket* (1951) and *Bad for Each Other* (1953). [See also pages 53, 87, 90, 100-101, 137.]

Below, Scott in the Technicolor noir *Desert Fury* with Burt Lancaster as Sheriff Tom Hanson.

Opposite, one of many poses while under contract to Hal Wallis.

At the roulette table with Bogart and Morris Carnavsky as Martinell in *Dead Reckoning*.

Two noirs with Charlton Heston. In *Bad for Each Other* (1953) Scott is heiress Helen Curtis in love with Heston's Dr. Tom Owen. Opposite, as torch singer Fran Garlan in *Dark City,* (1950).

As the ruthless Jane Palmer Scott gets the drop on Don Blanchard (Don DeFore) and sister-in-law Kathy (Kristine Miller) in *Too Late for Tears.* Below, flanked by Van Heflin as Sam and Barbara Stanwyck as the title character in *The Strange Love of Martha Ivers*.

More faces of Scott: with Kirk Douglas as mobster boyfriend Noll Turner in *I Walk Alone.* Below, again a torch singer and moll being pressured for information by Robert Mitchum as Capt. McQuigg in *The Racket* (1951).

Barbara Stanwyck

If for nothing other than the treacherous black widow Phyllis Dietrichson in *Double Indemnity* (see page 52), Barbara Stanwyck became the key prototype of the fatal woman in all of film noir. No stranger to playing strong women in her career stretching back into the 1930s, Stanwyck continued that trajectory through the noir period with other females who fought the stifling control of men around them, from *The Strange Love of Martha Ivers* or with Bogart in *The Two Mrs. Carrolls* (1947) to Robert Siodmak's *The File on Thelma Jordon* (1950), Anthony Mann's noir Western *The Furies* (1950), and Gerd Oswald's *Crime of Passion* (1957). [See also page 59.]

Below, Stanwyck as the title character concealing her crime with the help of assistant District Attorney Cleve Marshall (Wendell Corey) in *The FIle on Thelma Jordon.* Opposite, holding her own against both Kirk Douglas and Van Heflin in *The Strange Love of Martha Ivers* (see also page 218)

Facing off against Walter Huston as her domineering father in *The Furies* and, below, Bogart in *The Two Mrs. Carrolls.*

Above, Fred MacMurray's Neff admires the "honey of anklet" worn by Stanwyck as Phyllis in *Double Indemnity.*

With John Lund as Bill Harkness in *No Man of Her Own* (1950) based on the Cornell Woolrich *I Married a Dead Man.*

Later noir: as Helen Stillwin cajoling tough-guy Ralph Meeker as escaped convict Lawson in *Jeopardy* (1953).

In *Witness to Murder* (1953) Stanwyck's Cheryl Draper knows that George Sanders as Albert Richter has a body in that trunk; but the police won't believe her.

Below, as newspaperwoman Kathy Ferguson meeting police Captain Alidos (Royal Dano) and Lt. Bill Doyle (Sterling Hayden, right) whom she will marry in *Crime of Passion*.

Gene Tierney

Gene Tierney utilized her sloe-eyed, exotic beauty to create several landmark noir femme fatales. Josef von Sternberg, Marlene Dietrich's director in their remarkable series of 1930s films, was the first one to tap into the dark sensuality and deep psychological wells within Tierney in *The Shanghai Gesture* (see page 51). Tierney plays Poppy, the spoiled and rebellious daughter of the uptight businessman (Walter Huston). In defiance of him Poppy sinks into the world of depravity, sex, and drugs with the help of her Arab lover (Victor Mature). In Otto Preminger's *Laura* (see also pages 39 and 89) the femme fatale myth is turned on its head. Although all the obsessive men in the story see the supposedly dead Laura as a fatal lady, once she finally appears in the movie the viewer gradually realizes she is simply a level-headed ambitious career woman who would not submit to the narratives of her putative lovers. In *Leave Her to Heaven* (see also pages 34, 35, and 68), Tierney creates one of the most cold-blooded, psychopathic femme fatales in the annals of American cinema.

Below, *Whirlpool* (1949), the first of three sympathetic characters in successive noir films, Tierney's Ann Sutton is menaced by murderous hypnotherapist David Korvo (Jose Ferrer). Opposite, as Laura after being interrogated by Det. McPherson (Dana Andrews).

Shanghai Gesture: as the substance-abusing Victoria Charteris also known as Poppy next to Ona Munson as "Mother" Gin Sling.

Quite unlike *Leave Her to Heaven*'s sociopathic Ellen (opposite with Cornel Wilde as her duped husband Richard Hartland), both Mary Bristol in *Night and the City* (1950) and Morgan Taylor In *Where the Sidewalk Ends* (1950) Tierney's sympathetic characters tend to the physical injuries of criminal figures, Richard Widmark as grifter Harry Fabian and. opposite, Dana Andrews as rogue cop Mark Dixon.

Lana Turner

Lana Turner, one of the glamour queens of the American cinema, carved out a niche in the fatal woman pantheon with a single performance as Cora Smith (see also pages 36 and 128-129) in the first US adaptation of James Cain's *The Postman Always Rings Twice*. Her expression of the emotional complexities of the conflicted Cora remain quite remarkable and endlessly influential, as Turner effortlessly incarnates the ambition and the sexual hunger of Cain's protagonist. [See also page 61.]

Opposite, Turner as Cora proffers a cigarette to John Garfield as the severely injured Frank Chambers in *The Postman Always Rings Twice.*

Below, as socialite Lisbeth Bard, who falls for the head of a gambling syndicate, Robert Taylor, as the title character in the early noir *Johnny Eager* (1941).

The B List

> I hope they don't hang you, precious, by that sweet neck. Yes, angel, I'm gonna send you over. The chances are you'll get off with life. That means if you're a good girl, you'll be out in 20 years.
>
> *The Maltese Falcon*

Mary Astor

Even though Mary Astor may seem like a fatal woman in publicity stills (see also page 115), she is the definition of a one-shot, notable only for her performance as the femme fatale in the seminal 1941 *The Maltese Falcon* opposite the iconic Humphrey Bogart (below and also page 45) and based on noir literary giant Dashiell Hammett's novel. Even in that classic role, she has little agency or sensuality compared with her prototype (played by Bebe Daniels) in the earlier adaptation (1931) of Hammett's novel.

Ann Blyth

In the classic noir *Mildred Pierce* it is not the star Joan Crawford who is the femme fatale (in fact Crawford rarely played a femme fatale), it is her teenage daughter Veda, played by Ann Blyth. She is the spoiled, petulant daughter that Mildred caters to and who ultimately steals her second husband (Zachary Scott) and then in a fit murders him.

Below, *Brute Force* (1947) in which the petite Blyth is Ruth, the love interest of Burt Lancaster's character, inmate Joe Collins. Opposite, pleading with Zachary Taylor as the disdainful Monte Beragon in *Mildred Pierce.*

Leslie Brooks

In her truncated career model-actress Leslie Brooks played an outstanding femme fatale in a low-budget movie called *Blonde Ice* (1948). The title says it all. As society reporter Claire Cummings, Brooks wreaks havoc in the lives of numerous men who fall for her deceptions and seductions.

With elegant coiffure and double strand of pearls, Brooks poses with a shiny knife in a publicity portrait for *Blonde Ice*; but she actually prefers a gun as she repeatedly murders men and tries to frame her ex-lover Les Burns portrayed by Robert Paige, opposite top. Also in 1948 Brooks appeared as the girlfriend of Dr. Emil Bartok in *Hollow Triumph* (aka *The Scar*) but she is being manhandled by mobster John Muller (Paul Henreid in a dual role), who stole Bartok's identity.

Laraine Day

Laraine Day's performance in *The Locket* (1946) is a remarkable tour de force. German émigré director John Brahm crafts a complex structure that interweaves three-deep layers of flashbacks from the points of view of multiple, unreliable narrators. In this regard, *The Locket* is not only as modernist a film as *Citizen Kane* but also an examination of patriarchal desire to control the narrative. Female protagonists are uncommon in classic period noir, but many of them defy societal structures and traditional roles. Day's performance makes the afflicted woman in *The Locket*, who is basically uncontrollable as a kleptomanic, liar, and possible sociopath, relatable and sypathetic.

Below, at the bar: Day as Nan Collins, who has wed Brad (Robert Ryan) in the socially conscious noir *I Married A Communist* (1949, aka *The Woman on Pier 13*).

Opposite, as the deeply disturbed woman with many names, Nancy Fuller Monks Blair Patton, in *The Locket*.

The Locket: in the studio of her artist boyfriend Norman Clyde (Robert Mitchum) Nancy meets her future husband Dr. Harry Blair (Brian Aherne).

Day portrayed Edwina Brown (left), a socialite who survives an attack by a serial killer in the early noir *Fingers at the Window* (1942, with Lew Ayres). Top, as murderous housewife Jane Bandle with Franchot Tone as her lover and soon to be victim in *Without Honor* (1949, aka *The Woman Accused*).

Yvonne De Carlo

Yvonne De Carlo will always be remembered for her only significant fatal woman role in the classic film noir *Criss Cross* (see also page 107). She leads the obsessed protagonist played by Burt Lancaster through the seedy side streets of downtown Los Angeles to the shores of Palos Verdes where they both meet their doom at the hands of her gangster husband. [See also page 44.]

Opposite, as Anna with Burt Lancaster as ex-husband Steve Thompson, confronted by the man they have betrayed in *Criss Cross*. Below, *Brute Force*: as Gina Ferrara in a flashback with Howard Duff as "Soldier" Becker.

Veronica Lake

Although Veronica Lake appeared in several important film noirs like *This Gun for Hire* (1942) and *The Blue Dahlia* (1946, see also page 84), she never projected the agency and aggressiveness required of a fatal lady, with one exception—the noir Western *Ramrod* (1947), directed by then husband Andre de Toth. As the willful Connie, Lake refused to let any man determine her destiny, from her father down to her lovers. (See also page 60.)

Lake is posed pensively with Alan Ladd as the hit man Raven in *This Gun for Hire*. Opposite as Connie Dickason who uses her charm to manipulate Joel McCrea as Dave Nash to take on Preston Foster as cattle baron Frank Ivey in *Ramrod*.

Barbara Payton

Perhaps best remembered for her own fatal-woman lifestyle, her dangerous romantic relationships with fellow performers, especially noir actors Franchot Tone and Tom Neal, anchored her notorious autobiography *I Am Not Ashamed*. Payton's best-known shot as a deadly blonde was the one she put into her brother's ex-partner gangster James Cagney in *Kiss Tomorrow Goodbye*.

After the scandalous Payton/Tone/Neal triangle derailed her studio career, Payton made a few low-budget movies in the UK including the British noir *The Flanagan Boy* (much better known as *Bad Blonde*). Her last picture was the poverty-row noir for Edgar G. Ulmer *Murder is my Beat* (1955, aka *Danger is my Beat*).

Opposite, Payton posing provocatively in gown and fur for a studio portrait.

Below, as Holiday Charleton menaced by Cagney as low-rent shakedown artist Ralph Cotter in *Kiss Tomorrow Goodbye*.

Payton as Holiday watches with slight astonishment as rogue cops Lt. Reece (Barton MacLane, left) and Inspector Webber (Ward Bond) run their own shakedown and rough up Cotter in *Kiss Tomorrow Goodbye.*

Trapped: cigarette-girl Payton as Meg Dixon/Laurie Fredericks selling Chesterfields to John Hoyt as under-cover treasury agent Hackett.

Payton as singer Eden Lanei with smitten Det. Ray Patrick (Paul Langton) who is trying to clear her of a murder charge in *Murder is my Beat*.

A seductive pose in a publicity still for Warner Bros.

Gaby Rodgers

Posing as Lily Carver but actually Gabrielle, Gaby Rodgers portrays a character who is willing to open "Pandora's box" (in this case full of unstable nuclear material--see page 43 above) and "blow up the world" in Robert Aldrich's modernist apocalyptic film noir *Kiss Me Deadly*. Her greed, duplicity, and innocent façade give even the worldly private detective Mike Hammer a run for his money.

Although she did early television Rodgers would arguably be noir's most memorable one-shot fatal woman, except for her other credit in *The Big Break* (1953), a quirky, no-budget riff on *The Naked City* (both the 1948 movie and the Arthur "Weegee" Fellig book)

Opposite, Rodgers poses with a revolver: an alternate to the scene when Hammer enters her hotel room on Page 79 above.

Below, Rodgers as Gabrielle/Lily Carver reads Christina Rossetti's poem "Remember" to an attentive Ralph Meeker as Mike Hammer.

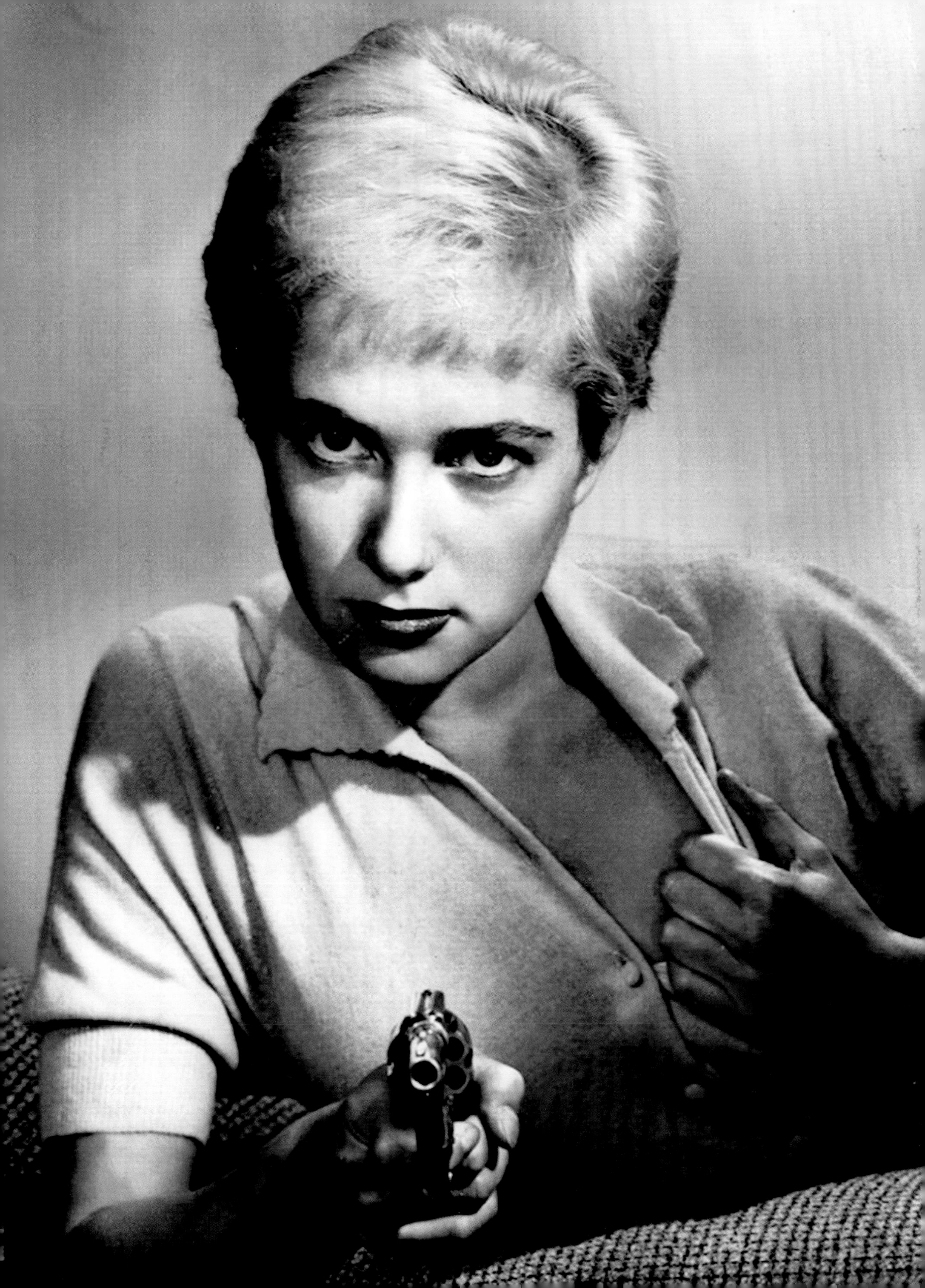

Ann Savage

Ann Savage's fatal woman reputation is built almost entirely on one film, Edgar G. Ulmer's cult noir *Detour*. Her performance as Vera is among the most unsympathetic of femme fatales in noir. Her humiliation of the hapless protagonist Al Roberts (Tom Neal) is unrelenting, as is her ability to control the narrative of the film once she appears.

Savage was sometimes as a scheming fatal women as in *Apology for Murder* (1945, originally scripted by Edgar G. Ulmer as *Single Indemnity*, which gives away its derivative plot line) or other times a relatively innocent reporter, girlfriend, sister, etc. With *The Spider* (1945), *Midnight Manhun*t (1945), *The Last Crooked Mile* (1946), *Lady Killer* (1947), *Pier 23* (1951), Savage made a half dozen other noirs mostly for Poverty Row and almost always with a signature sneer. [See also page 116.]

Below, Savage as Vera and Neal as Al Roberts. Her expression of disdain and his baleful stare of unrelenting dismay are visual constants in almost every scene. Opposite, only slightly less menacing in a 1944 glamour portrait for Paramount.

An unusual look for Savage in another studio shot with upswept blond locks and a smile that is only slightly sinister.

Not exactly a honey of an anklet: Savage as Toni Kirkland, whose opinion of her older husband Harvey (Russell Hicks) is written all over her face in *Apology for Murder.*

Savage in her element, coffin nail in hand, wind in her hair, as she takes Al Roberts for a ride with the top down in *Detour.*

Another look from Savage, in a pill-box hat as Florence Cain in *The Spider,* gives pause even to the typically hardbitten Richard Conte as Chris Conlon.

Jean Simmons

Jean Simmons delivered her key fatal woman potrayal in *Angel Face*. In a typical play against type director Otto Preminger used Simmons' youthful, almost "angelic" looks to disguise the fact that her character, heiress Diane Tremayne, is a psychotic narcissist who is capable of murdering not only her parents but also her disaffected lover in a moment of self-immolation. [See also pages 62 and 96.]

Below, in a posed shot, Robert Mitchum as paramedic Frank Jesseup basks in the "angelic" glow of Simmons as Diane in *Angel Face.*

Opposite, the British period noir *Footsteps in the Fog* (1955): as blackmailing maid Lily Watkins seems suprised that her employer and would-be victim Stephen Lowry (Stewart Granger) is prepared to take her threat in hand literally.

Gloria Swanson

In the 1920s Gloria Swanson was no stranger to portraying a man-eating vamps if she needed to. In *Sunset Boulevard*, the underlying irony is created through those earlier characterizations. In Billy Wilder's Hollywood-gothic noir, Swanson is aging movie star Norma Desmond, who shares her decaying mansion with servant Max von Mayerling (Erich von Stroheim) who was once her director and paramour. Enter cynical screenwriter Joe Gillis (William Holden) who fails to see the threat posed by this sort of fatal woman. [See also page 48.]

Below, Swanson as Norma plays the pity card with Gillis. Opposite, Norma's celebrated lament for a more glorious celluloid past.

Audrey Totter

As Claire Quimby in *Tension* (1949), who inspires her cuckolded husband to plan her lover's murder, Audrey Totter fulfilled the fatal promise made when she danced with the devil (almost literally) in *Alias Nick Beal* [see pages 46 and 91]. Claire's outright rejection of life as a humdrum housewife living in a tract house reflects the hidden urges of many women in postwar American noir. Totter's other noir performances were less deadly but still not a standard heroine. In 1947 alone Totter was snide Marlowe foil Adrienne Fromsett in the quirky adaptation of *Lady in the Lake*, Dr. Ann Lorrison treating a disturbed veteran in *High Wall*, and victim Althea Keane in *The Unsuspected.* Besides *Tension* in 1949 Totter was the long-suffering wife in the boxing noir *The Setup* (1949) and a call girl in *Alias Nick Beal.* Her final noir was as ex-moll Joyce Geary being blackmailed in *A Bullet for Joey* (1955). Of course, Totter's first noir was as the brief distraction for Frank Chambers in *The Postman Always Rings Twice.*

Below, *Lady in the Lake*: Totter in actor/director Robert Montgomery's subjective-camera staging of Raymond Chandler's first-person novel.

Opposite, Totter's expression as Claire clutching her broken doll in *Tension* clearly bodes ill for some man.

Another posed shot clutching a man with a gun, this time George Raft as Joe Victor in *A Bullet for Joey.* Left, as brunette Madge Gorland in *The Postman Always Rings Twice.*

A posed shot from *High Wall*: Totter as Dr. Lorrison cowers next to gun-wielding Robert Taylor as Steven Kenet.

Opposite, Totter's expression says it all when Claire Quimby's husband Warren (Richard Basehart) drives her to see a tract house he wants to buy in *Tension.*

Claire Trevor

Certainly never to be forgotten for her incarnation of the impeccably coiffed, often bejewelled but still deadly socialite Helen Chandler, who is actually an escapee from a past life as low-rent moll Velma Valento in *Murder, My Sweet* (see also pages 41 and 122), Claire Trevor's other bad girls were more middle-class in *Born to Kill* (1948) and Anthony Mann's *Raw Deal* (1947).

Below, *Murder, My Sweet*: Trevor as the very wealthy and very deadly Helen Grayle with Dick Powell's Marlowe.

Opposite, Trevor as Pat Regan, girlfriend of an escaped convict in Anthony Mann's *Raw Deal* (1948).

Above, as Ruth Dillon with the amnesiac Frank Thompson (Burgess Meredith) in the adaptation of Cornell Woolrich's *Street of Chance* (1942). Below, as Terry Codell leaning over her boyfriend forger George Steele (Pat O'Brien) while art expert Traybin (Herbert Marshall) looks on.

Above, as new divorcee Helen Trent, rolling the dice before hooking up with stone-cold onlooker Sam Wilde (Lawrence Tierney) in *Born to Kill* (1947). Below, *Borderline* (1950): Trevor as policewoman Madeleine Haley, who is unaware that Fred MacMurray is also undercover as Johnny Macklin in Mexico meeting gangster Harvey Gumbin (Roy Roberts).

Alida Valli

As Maddalena Paradine, Alida Valli's imperious looks and classic beauty easily ensnare the hapless barrister Anthony Keane (Gregory Peck) in Hitchcock's *The Paradine Case* (1947). He ultimately fails to clear her of her husband's murder...because she is guilty. [See also page 48.]

The idealized lovers: Valli as Maddelena and Louis Jourdan as valet André Latour in *The Paradine Case.*

Martha Vickers

Martha Vickers plays the teen femme fatale Carmen (see page 78) in Howard Hawks' adaptation of *The Big Sleep*. She is a promiscuous Lolita with a taste for danger and drugs. Vickers last noir before transitioning to television work was the gun-toting Della (see page 69) in *The Burglar* (1957).

Below, *The Big Sleep*: Bogart discovers Vickers as Carmen high as a kite next to a body.

Opposite top, Vickers as teen runaway Kate Klinger, who has become torch singer Kitty Travers in *Alimony.* (1949). Bottom, as Susan Duane, the spurned fiancee of an unscrupulous businessman in Edgar G. Ulmer's *Ruthless* (1948).

Helen Walker

As Lilith—a name that is almost too much on the money—Helen Walker in *Nightmare Alley* (1947) portrays a psychiatrist who can out-huckster the chief con man of the piece, Stanton Carlisle. She is a commanding presence, particularly when dressed in a gender-coded "male" suit, making her seem even more androgynous.

Walker was also treacherous as Irene Williams, the adulterous wife plotting to kill her wealthy husband in *Impact* (1949, see page 124). Her last film appearance was as the alcoholic wife of mobster Mr. Brown in Joseph H. Lewis' *The Big Combo.* [See also page 84.]

Below, Walker as Dr. Lilith Ritter with Tyrone Power as Stanton Carlisle in *Nightmare Alley*. Opposite, studio portrait in gown with cigarette holder for *Impact*.

Marie Windsor

As the fatal woman in Stanley Kubrick's 1956 heist film *The Killing*, Marie Windsor projects ruthlessness and vulgarity in her humiliation of her submissive husband. She enlists the aid of her lover to cheat the band of thieves but ends up imploding the whole scheme.

Windsor made other noirs portraying a victim of the misogynistic title character in *The Sniper* (1952) and the wife of a mob boss in both *Force of Evil* (1948) and *The Narrow Margin* (1952). In *No Man's Woman* (1955), when Windsor's character Carol Ellenson Grant turns up murdered, investigators have to sort through a half-dozen suspects, from an estranged husband she was blackmailing to a woman whose fiance she stole. [See also pages 49 and 59.]

Below, Windsor as nightclub singer Jean Darr cajoling psychopathic delivery man Eddie Miller (Arthur Franz) into doing her a favor in *The Sniper.* That turns out to be a bad idea for Jean.

Opposite, a posed shot of Windsor as the gangster widow turned crass government witness en route to testify and under the protection of LAPD Det. Sgt. Walter Brown (Charles McGraw) in *The Narrow Margin.*

Windsor as the scheming Sherry Petty with her husband George (Elisha Cook, Jr.) in *The Killing.*

What Else You Got?

I don't go to church. Kneeling bags my nylons.

Ace in the Hole

At the major studios, noir films such as *Double Indemnity*, *Leave Her to Heaven*, and *The Letter* notwithstanding, stars such as Barbara Stanwyck at Paramount, Gene Tierney at 20th Century-Fox, or Bette Davis at Warner Bros. rarely portrayed cold-blooded killers. With the occasional exception, many of the fatal women who populate classic period film noir were incarnated by performers that were tagged with B, C, and even less premium letter designations. This was especially true in the low-budget titles produced by PRC, Eagle-Lion, Lippert, and other "poverty row" studios, where the likes of Ann Savage and Cleo Moore were stars.

Hot Spot: Frankie Christopher (Victor Mature) and Jill Lynn (Betty Grable) discover the body of Carole Landis as Vicky. Opposite, *Vicki*: Jean Peters as the hash-slinging title character is transformed into a popular singer.

At Fox, for example, *Hot Spot* (1941) and *Vicki* (1953), the two adaptations of Steve Fisher's hard-boiled novel *I Wake Up Screaming*, in which promoters make ill-fated waitress Vicki Lynn into a star and a fatal woman, the top-tier (and larger) role of sister Jill went to "good girls" Betty Grable and Jeanne Crain. Carole Landis and Jean Peters (see also page 139) ended up portraying the slightly venal murder victims who become the object of an investigator's obsession.

One way to split the difference between a good girl and a fatal woman was to concoct a tale of twins. In the best known example, *Dark Mirror*, Olivia de Havilland portrays Ruth Collins and her psychotic sibling Terry (she's the one with the disaffected look while smoking in bed below—see also page 65). Another pair of emotionally mismatched twins are portrayed by former child star Bonita Granville (who was 15 when cast in a series of "Nancy Drew" features) in *The Guilty* (1947).

Many instances of a single role in which a woman is atypically cast as deadly female also have mitigating elements in their plots. In *The Accused* (1949) when typically virtuous Loretta Young as college professor Wilma Tuttle is attacked by a male student, she beats him to death in self-defense then stages an accident to cover up what she did.

Above, *The Guilty*, Bonita Granville as the avaricious Estelle Mitchell, whose twin Linda was killed by Don Castle as Mike Carr thinking she was Estelle. Right, Bill Perry (Douglas Dick) plans to have his way with a startled Loretta Young as Professor Tuttle in *The Accused*.

Equally atypical casting is Ann Todd in the period noir *So Evil My Love* (1948). Immediately after appearing as the long-suffering wife of an obsessed barrister in *The Paradine Case*, Todd was cast as Olivia Harwood, the selfless widow of a missionary. Despite her upright past, Olivia's shipboard encounter with art thief Mark Bellis leads to an unfortunate infatuation, under the power of which she becomes both a blackmailer and a poisoner. Not to be outdone, the following year husband David Lean cast her as the notorious, real-life arsenic user, the title character in *Madeleine* (1950).

Below, Todd as Olivia nurses an ill Mark Bellis (Ray Milland) back to health in *So Evil, My Love*. Opposite, Todd as Madeleine Smith is seen concocting her deadly brew.

One more unexpected portrayal of a period fatal woman was in *Ivy* (1947) by Joan Fontaine, better known as an early Hitchcock blonde under threat in both *Rebecca* (1940) and *Suspicion* (1941). In an increasingly common noir plot, period or otherwise, Fontaine's Ivy Lexton is unhappily married to a man with limited prospects. Of course, when you're having an affair with a handsomer man and scheming to entrap a wealthier one as a second husband, a dose of arsenic is so much simpler than a divorce proceeding.

Opposite. Fontaine elegantly attired as Ivy, a fatal woman who sees no need to dress down even as she handles the contents of a bottle with a skull and crossbones on it.

Below, expressing some concerns but still well-coiffed, Fontaine emotes in a scene with her mother Lillian Fontaine as Lady Flora.

POISON

Above, Angela Lansbury as Myra with her snub-nosed revolver in *Please Murder Me!*

Below, Anne Baxter as Evelyn poses for Douglas Proctor (Ralph Bellamy), her fiance's brother in *Guest in the House.*

British emigre Angela Lansbury's noir debut was the Cockney maid in *Gaslight*. While that was not an entirely sympathetic character, Lansbury never portrayed a killer until she was cast against type as the scheming divorcee Myra Leeds in *Please Murder Me!* (1956).

Others who were ingenues in the 1940s seldom if ever crossed over to portray fatal women. Anne Baxter was a self-described "idealized girl next door." Arguably Baxter's most memorable performances were the fallen woman in *The Razor's Edge* (1946) and the malicious title character in *All About Eve* (1950), but in *Guest in the House* (1944) her character Evelyn Heath is a pure femme fatale masquerading as an ingenuous invalid, who schemes to trade in her gullible fiance for his worldlier older brother.

In the early 1950s, Mickey Rooney starred in two B-budget noirs at MGM and Columbia that hinge on his character falling for a seemingly wholesome but fatal young woman. Both Sally Forrest in *The Strip* (1951) and Dianne Foster in *Drive A Crooked Road* (1954) had youthful looks that belied their intentions. In *The Strip*, Forrest's cigarette girl /dancer Jane Maxton is brought down by her overweening ambition to become a star.

With a plot liberally borrowed from *The Killers,* in *Drive A Crooked Road* Foster's Barbara Matthews (above) ultimately regrets her manipulation of Rooney's driver/mechanic Eddie Shannon but too late for a happy ending.

Also in the early 1950s, Beverly Michaels was certainly no ingenue in two low-budget noirs inspired by *The Postman Always Rings Twice*: *Pickup* (1951) and *Wicked Woman* (1953).

Standing in for Cleo Moore to co-star with *Pickup* director Hugo Haas, as the older husband and would be victim, Michaels' Betty is every bit as slutty as the stereotypical pose at left suggests.

In *Wicked Woman* (aka *Free and Easy*) Michaels' Billie Nash gets off a bus and lands a job at a local bar (see page 94). After seducing the owner Matt Bannister (Richard Egan, with Michaels opposite) Billie wants him to dump his alcoholic wife, empty the safe, and run off with her. That doesn't work out, so Billie ends up back on the bus.

Columbia contract player Janis Carter had a score of B-budget credits before portraying a socialite who witnesses a murder in *Night Editor* (1946), first episode of a series of features that never materialized. Her next feature was *Framed* (1947). As the triple-timing Paula Craig, Carter is a blond barmaid who helps set up Mike Lambert (Glenn Ford with Carter at right) to be killed only to do in her embezzler boyfriend and frame Mike for that.

As a nightclub singer named Alice in *Body and Soul* (1947) South African actress Hazel Brooks was little more than a social climber looking to spend money provided by boxer Charley Davis. The following year in *Sleep, My Love* (1948), she is involved in a plot to drive an inconvenient wife insane.

In a mere eight years Jan Sterling's career in film noir included a dozen titles: *Union Station*, *Appointment with Danger* (both 1950), *Flesh and Fury* (1952), *Split Second* (1953), *Female on the Beach* (1955), *The Harder They Fall* (1956), and *The Female Animal* (1958). She also did two stretches inside in *Caged* (1950) and *Women's Prison* (1955). She was a hard-bitten "working girl" in both *Mystery Street* (1950) and *The Human Jungle* (see pages 121 and 140-141). But no character was more memorable or deadlier than the faithless Lorraine Minosa, who stabs reporter Chuck Tatum in *Ace in the Hole* (1951).

Below, Brooks as Alice with John Garfield as Charley Davis in *Body and Soul.*
Opposite, watching as fake psychiatrist Vernay (George Couloris) bends on the fallen Bruce Elcott in *Sleep, My Love.*

BUTLER
APTS

Above, Jan Sterling as B-girl Vivian Heldon in *Mystery Street* (1950). Below, attacked by Kirk Douglas as Tatum in *Ace in the Hole.*

Sterling poses defiantly in a grimy cell as "Smoochie" in *Caged* and sports much the same look as Brenda (inset) in *Women's Prison.*

Early in her career Ann Sheridan was a wholesome good girl in the proto noirs *They Made Me a Criminal* (1939) and *They Drive By Night* (1940, see pages 51 and 196). She is merely accused of being a fatal woman as the adulterous wife Chris Hunter in *The Unfaithful* (1947). As the nightclub singer and title figure in *Nora Prentiss* (1947) she does precipitate the destruction of Dr. Richard Talbot (see page 126). Opposite, she is again a title character in *Woman on the Run* (1950, see also page 94). [See also pages 48, 56, and 117.]

Sometimes the only way to confront a fatal woman is with a gat: Alan Ladd as Johnny Morrison aims his service pistol at Doris Dowling as his faithless Helen in *Blue Dahlia*.

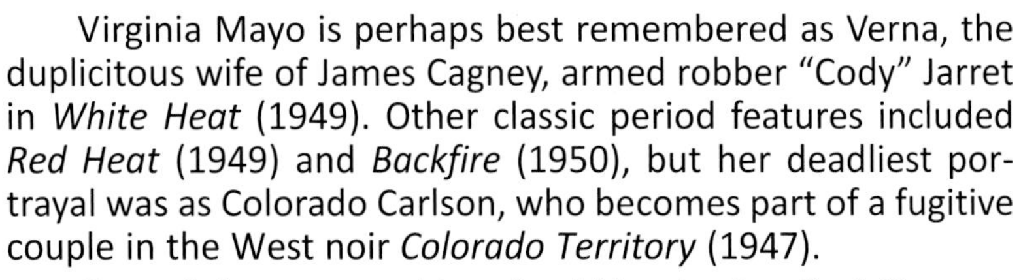

Virginia Mayo is perhaps best remembered as Verna, the duplicitous wife of James Cagney, armed robber "Cody" Jarret in *White Heat* (1949). Other classic period features included *Red Heat* (1949) and *Backfire* (1950), but her deadliest portrayal was as Colorado Carlson, who becomes part of a fugitive couple in the West noir *Colorado Territory* (1947).

One of the most ruthless fatal blondes in all of film noir was Margot Shelby portrayed by British actress Jean Gillie. Margot's tawdry story is told in flashback in *Decoy* (1946).

Opposite, bottom, another threesome in the front seat: Jean Gillie as Margot is flanked by Jim Vincent (Edward Norris with the gun) and Dr. Lloyd Craig (Hubert Rudley). Shortly she will run Vincent over with the car and shoot the doctor.

Colorado Territory: As Colorado Mayo packs two guns (left) and poses provocatively with Joel McCrea as outlaw Wes McQueen.

Given that Cody really only had eyes for Ma (Margaret Wycherly seated between her daughter-in-law and Sonny-boy), the expression on Verna's face is understandable.

In their seminal study *Panorama du Film Noir Américain*, Raymond Borde and Étienne Chaumeton singled out *Kiss Me Deadly* (with typical French understatement) as "the fascinating twilight of film noir, a desperate mirror of how the movement began...with a savage lyricism that hurls us into a world in full decay, ruled by the cruel and the sexually depraved." In fact, *Kiss Me Deadly* is just as much a beginning of the classic period's second act, full of men who were even more anti-heroic and women who were even more fatal.

Besides Gaby Rodgers as the duplicitous Lily Carver, *Kiss Me Deadly* had three other women in supporting roles (at right): Cloris Leachman as the doomed Christina (naked under a trenchcoat and tortured to death in the movie but happily striking a cheesecake pose on the left); Marian Carr as the end-of-the-work-week moll Friday (looking apprehensively over a spaghetti-strapped shoulder); and Maxine Cooper as the durable Velda (who, after all, drags the wounded Hammer out of the exploding beach house).

Only Carr had previously established femme fatale credentials. In director Robert Aldrich's earlier *World for Ransom*, it was Carr with the odd but onomatopoeically apt name of Frennessey, whose lesbianism is about as well concealed as her arms and bodice under a black negligee. Her cool sexuality easily bends the behavior of the hapless Mike Callahan (Dan Duryea, posed with Carr, below) to her will.

Det. Diamond (Cornell Wilde, below) is almost undone by his desperate obsession with the disaffected moll Susan Lowell (Jean Wallace) in *The Big Combo.*

Opposite, as duplicitous secretary Meta Carson, Rhonda Fleming's first noir was no less than *Out of the Past.*

Ruth Roman displays two faces of the femme fatale in *Tomorrow Is Another Day* (1951). She enmeshes the developmentally arrested Bill Clark (Steve Cochran, above) as blond taxi-dancer "Cay" Higgins (under threat of a gun in the inset above right) but transforms into a wifely brunette after they become a fugitive couple.

Lucille Ball is certainly not famous for her work in noir. Nonetheless it was more than a one-shot. There is not a lot of fatality in her portrayal of *The Dark Corner's* loyal secretary (see also pages 104 and 132), in the prototypical style established by Ella Raines' Kansas in *Phantom Lady*; but her earlier films for RKO include the paralyzed and manipulative ex-singer in *The Big Street* (1942) and John Farrow's Nick-Musuraca-photographed *Five Came Back* (1939).

Like Roman in *Tomorrow Is Another Day*, Ball stars as a taxi dancer in *Lured* (1947, see also page 88), who again like Kansas works with a police inspector to prove the innocence of a man she loves.

Below, Ball with Joseph Calleia as the mysterious Moyani in *Lured*. Opposite, a doppelgänger glamour pose typical of fatal women.

Undoubtedly best known for the shrill-voiced silent star in *Singin' in the Rain* (1952), Jean Hagen also graced several noir films, most notably leading Joe Norson (Farley Granger) into a trap as singer Harriet Sinton in *Side Street* (1950) and as girlfriend "Doll" Conovan, who is part of the fatalistic chain of events in *The Asphalt Jungle* that dooms Dix Handley (Sterling Hayden, opposite top, with Hagen eyeing a stone and Sam Jaffe as caper-meister "Doc" Riedenschneider).

Dorothy Malone is most closely associated with the troubled blondes she portrayed in 1950s melodramas for director Douglas Sirk. She was also a blonde, the kidnapped half of a fugitive couple, in the original *The Fast and the Furious,* a very low-budget noir produced by Roger Corman, and Don Siegel's *Private Hell 36* (both 1954). But Malone's most famous noir character may be the bespectacled, book-selling brunette who helps Bogart's Marlowe in *The Big Sleep* (opposite bottom).

SECTION C
ENGINEERING
NOVELS

Although, in portraying the innocent Molly, Coleen Gray might be considered a party to Stanton Carlisle's descent into madness in *Nightmare Alley*, she is a positive figure as the long-suffering wife in *Kiss of Death* (1947). As the equally long-suffering fiancée Fay in *The Killing,* she is the antithesis of Marie Windsor's Sherry Peatty (see page 280), when she urges Sterling Hayden's Johnny to save himself.

In *The Sleeping City* (1950), however, as nurse-turned-drug-mule Ann Sebastian, Gray's criminal character is ultimately thrown over in the manner of Spade with Brigid Shaughnessy by Richard Conte's Fred Rowan.

Below, Gray with Conte in *The Sleeping City*. Opposite, *Nightmare Alley*: looking apprehensive while in the clutches of Tyrone Power as Stanton Carlisle.

As an ingénue Gail Russell was "introduced" in the role of the emotionally bereft Stella ("by starlight," as per the movie's song) in Paramount's unexpected wartime hit *The Uninvited* (1944). She was the only actor who returned for the unofficial sequel *The Unseen* (1945), a convoluted mystery that not even a polish by Raymond Chandler could straighten out. In Frank Borzage's elegiac *Moonrise* Russell's teenaged Gilly tries to help the hapless Danny Hawkins from repeating the sins of his murderer father. Saving Jean Courtland, Russell's character in the adaptation of Cornell Woolrich's *Night Has a Thousand Eyes*, is the underlying reason for the self-immolation of Edward G. Robinson's John Triton, but only the post-ingénue Russell is inarguably fatal as Carol Morrow (below), when she shoots her sheriff boyfriend on the steps of a courthouse at the end of *The Tattered Dress* (1957).

Right, Russell looking innocent and menaced in *The Unseen.* Opposite, with Dane Clark as Danny in *Moonrise.*

Arguably the youngest and oldest actors to portray a woman leading a film noir double life were Deanna Durbin and Joan Crawford. In fact, Durbin (who began her career as MGM's second singing teenager, after Judy Garland) did it twice in her only noir films. The alter ego in *Lady on a Train* is innocent enough: Durbin's debutante Nicki Collins witnesses a murder and while investigating on her own is mistaken for singer Margo Martin (see page 96). A bleaker motive drives Durbin's character in *Christmas Holiday* (1944): blamed by her husband's family after he is convicted of murder, Abigail Manette becomes hostess and entertainer Jackie Lamont for a brothel in New Orleans.

While certainly better remembered for *Mildred Pierce* (see pages 68 and 77) or the menaced Myra Hudson in *Sudden Fear* (1952), Joan Crawford's dual role In *The Damned Don't Cry* (1950) takes her from Texas, where she abandons her husband after the death of her son, to New York. There Ethel Whitehead becomes Lorna Hansen, a courtesan/moll, who double-crosses one mobster after falling for another.

Opposite, Deanna Durbin as Abigail is confronted by her husband, Robert (Gene Kelly), in *Christmas Holiday.*

Below, accountant Martin Blackford (Kent Smith) coaches Joan Crawford's Lorna Hansen on how to seduce one of his mobster clients in *The Damned Don't Cry*.

Index of Illustrations